THE ULTIMATE
$\mathcal{F}$AT - $\mathcal{F}$REE
COOKBOOK

THE ULTIMATE
Fat-Free
COOKBOOK

CONSULTANT EDITOR ANNE SHEASBY

LORENZ BOOKS

This Edition published by Lorenz Books
an imprint of
Anness Publishing Limited
Hermes House, 88-89 Blackfriars Road
London SE1 8HA

A CIP catalogue record for this book is available from the British Library

ISBN 0-7548-0406-2

Publisher: Joanna Lorenz
Senior Editor: Linda Fraser
Designer: Sara Kidd
Photographers: Karl Adamson, Steve Baxter, Amanda Heywood, Michael Michaels, Don Last,
Edward Allwright, Thomas Odulate, James Duncan, Peter Reilly, Patrick McLeavey
Recipes: Carla Capalbo and Laura Washburn, Stephen Wheeler, Christine France, Shirley Gill,
Roz Denny, Annie Nichols, Linda Fraser, Catherine Atkinson, Maggie Pannell,
Kit Chan, Sue Maggs, Christine Ingram
Home Economists: Wendy Lee, Jane Stevenson, Elizabeth Wolf Cohen,
Kit Chan assisted by Lucy McKelvie, Kathryn Hawkins
Stylists: Blake Minton and Kirsty Rawlings, Fiona Tillett, Hilary Guy,
Thomas Odulate, Madeleine Brehaut, Jo Harris

Printed and bound in Singapore

© 1997 Anness Publishing Limited
Updated © 2000
3 5 7 9 10 8 6 4 2

NOTES
For all recipes, quantities are given in both metric and imperial measures and, where appropri-
ate, measures are also given in standard cups and spoons. Follow one set, but not a mixture
because they are not interchangeable.

Standard spoon and cup measures are level.

1 tsp = 5ml, 1 tbsp = 15ml, 1 cup = 8fl oz/250ml.

Medium eggs should be used unless otherwise stated.

CONTENTS

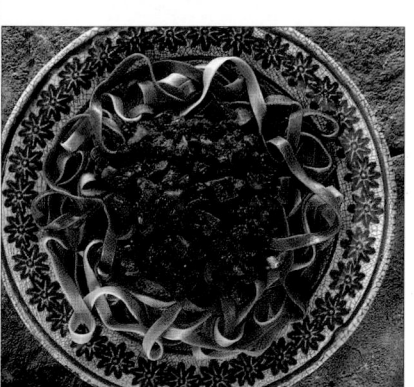

INTRODUCTION

Cooking and eating good food is one of life's greatest pleasures – and there's nothing wrong with enjoying good food, except that for too long good often meant fatty. Butter, oil, cheese and other fatty foods were considered essential for good cooking. We know now that all this fat – along with too much sugar and salt – has a huge impact on health.

Most of us eat fats in one form or another every day. In fact, we need to consume a small amount of fat to maintain a healthy and balanced diet, but almost everyone can afford to, and should, reduce their fat intake, particularly of saturated fats. Weight for weight, dietary fats supply far more energy than all the other nutrients in our diet. If you eat a diet that is high in fats and don't exercise enough to use up that energy, you will put on weight. By cutting down on fat, you can easily reduce your energy intake without affecting the other essential nutrients. And by choosing the right types of fat, using low fat and fat-free products whenever possible, and making small, simple changes to the way you cook and prepare food, you can reduce your overall fat intake quite dramatically and enjoy a much healthier diet without really noticing any difference.

As you will see, watching your fat intake doesn't have to mean dieting and deprivation. *The Ultimate Fat-Free Cookbook* opens with an informative introduction about basic healthy eating guidelines – you'll find out about the five main food groups, and how, by simply choosing a variety of foods from these groups every

day, you can ensure that you are eating all the nutrients you need. One way to enjoy your favourite foods without guilt is to substitute lower fat ingredients for higher fat ones. This book will introduce you to these lower fat ingredients and show you how to use them. There are hints and tips on how to cook with fat-free and low fat ingredients; techniques for using healthy, fat-free fruit purée in place of butter or margarine in all your favourite baking recipes; suggestions for which foods to cut down on and what to try instead; easy ways to reduce fat and saturated fat in your foods; new no fat and low fat cooking techniques and information on the best cookware for fat-free cooking; along with a delicious section on low fat and very low fat snacks.

There are over 200 easy-to-follow recipes for delicious dishes that your whole family can enjoy. Every recipe has been developed to fit into modern nutritional guidelines, and each one has at-a-glance nutritional information so you can instantly check the calories and fat content. The recipes are very low in fat – all contain less than five grams of fat per serving and many contain less than one. The selection of foods included will surprise you: there are barbecues and bakes, pizza and pastas, tasty sautés and stews, vegetable dishes and vegetarian main courses, fish and seafood dishes galore and delicious breads, biscuits and cakes. All without as much fat as traditional recipes, of course, but packed with flavour and vitality.

Fresh vegetables and pulses (far left) and fresh fruit (left and above) make ideal choices for fat-free and low fat cooking.

HEALTHY EATING GUIDELINES

A healthy diet is one that provides the body with all the nutrients it needs to be able to grow and repair properly. By eating the right types, balance and proportions of foods, we are more likely to feel healthy, have plenty of energy and a higher resistance to illness that will help protect our body against developing diseases such as heart disease, cancers, bowel disorders and obesity.

By choosing a variety of foods every day, you will ensure that you are supplying your body with all the essential nutrients, including vitamins and minerals, it needs. To get the balance right, it is important to know just how much of each type of food you should be eating.

There are five main food groups (see right), and it is recommended that we should eat plenty of fruit, vegetables (at least five portions a day, not including potatoes) and foods such as cereals,

pasta, rice and potatoes; moderate amounts of meat, fish, poultry and dairy products; and only small amounts of foods containing fat or sugar. By choosing a good balance of foods from these groups every day, and choosing lower fat or lower sugar alternatives wherever possible, we will be supplying our bodies with all the nutrients they need for optimum health.

THE ROLE AND IMPORTANCE OF FAT IN OUR DIET

Fats shouldn't be cut out of our diets completely. We need a small amount of fat for general health and well-being – fat is a valuable source of energy, and also helps to make foods more palatable to eat. However, if you lower the fats, especially saturated fats, in your diet, you will feel healthier; it will help you lose weight and reduce the risk of developing some diseases.

THE FIVE MAIN FOOD GROUPS

● Fruit and vegetables

● Rice, potatoes, bread, pasta and other cereals

● Meat, poultry, fish and alternative proteins

● Milk and other dairy foods

● Foods which contain fat and foods which contain sugar

Aim to limit your daily intake of fats to no more than 30% of total calories. In real terms, this means that for an average intake of 2,000 calories per day, 30% of energy would come from 600 calories. Since each gram of fat provides 9 calories, your total daily intake should be no more than 66.6g fat. Your total intake of saturated fats should be no more than 10% of the total calories.

TYPES OF FAT

All fats in our foods are made up of building blocks of fatty acids and glycerol and their properties vary according to each combination.

There are two types of fat – saturated and unsaturated. The unsaturated group is divided into two types – polyunsaturated and monounsaturated fats.

There is always a combination of each of the three types of fat (saturated, polyunsaturated and monounsaturated fats) in any food, but the amount of each type varies greatly from one food to another.

Left: By choosing a variety of foods from the five main food groups, you will ensure that you are supplying your body with all the nutrients it needs.

SATURATED FATS

All fatty acids are made up of chains of carbon atoms. Each atom has one or more free "bonds" to link with other atoms and by doing so the fatty acids transport nutrients to cells throughout the body. Without these free "bonds" the atom cannot form any links, that is to say it is completely "saturated". Because of this, the body finds it hard to process the fatty acid into energy, so it simply stores it as fat.

Saturated fats are the fats which you should reduce, as they can increase the level of cholesterol in the blood, which in turn can increase the risk of developing heart disease.

The main sources of saturated fats are animal products, such as meat, and fats, such as butter and lard that are solid at room temperature. However, there are also saturated fats of vegetable origin, notably coconut and palm oils, and some margarines and oils, which are processed by changing some of the unsaturated fatty acids to saturated ones – they are labelled "hydrogenated vegetable oil" and should be avoided.

POLYUNSATURATED FATS

There are two types of polyunsaturated fats, those of vegetable or plant origin (omega 6), such as sunflower oil, soft margarine and seeds, and those from oily fish (omega 3), such as herring, mackerel and sardines. Both fats are usually liquid at room temperature. Small quantities of polyunsaturated fats are essential for good health and are thought to help reduce the level of cholesterol in the blood.

MONOUNSATURATED FATS

Monounsaturated fats are also thought to have the beneficial effect of reducing the blood cholesterol level and this could explain why in some

Above: A selection of foods containing the three main types of fat found in foods.

Mediterranean countries there is such a low incidence of heart disease. Monounsaturated fats are found in foods such as olive oil, rapeseed oil, some nuts such as almonds and hazelnuts, oily fish and avocado pears.

CUTTING DOWN ON FATS AND SATURATED FATS IN THE DIET

About one quarter of the fat we eat comes from meat and meat products, one-fifth from dairy products and margarine and the rest from cakes, biscuits, pastries and other foods. It is easy to cut down on obvious sources of fat in the diet, such as butter, oils, margarine, cream, whole milk and full fat cheese, but we also need to know

about – and watch out for – "hidden" fats. Hidden fats can be found in foods such as cakes, biscuits and nuts. Even lean, trimmed red meats may contain as much as 10% fat.

By being aware of foods which are high in fats and particularly saturated fats, and by making simple changes to your diet, you can reduce the total fat content of your diet quite considerably. Whenever possible, choose reduced fat or low fat alternatives to foods such as milk, cheese and salad dressings, and fill up on very low fat foods, such as fruit and vegetables, and foods that are high in carbohydrate such as pasta, rice, bread and potatoes.

EASY WAYS TO CUT DOWN FAT AND SATURATED FAT IN THE DAILY DIET

There are lots of simple no-fuss ways of reducing the fat in your diet. Just follow the simple "eat less – try instead" suggestions below to discover how easy it is.

● EAT LESS – Butter, margarine and hard fats.

● TRY INSTEAD – Low fat spread, very low fat spread or polyunsaturated margarine. If you must use butter or hard margarine, make sure they are softened at room temperature and spread them very thinly. Better still, use fat-free spreads such as low fat soft cheese, reduced sugar jams or marmalades for sandwiches and toast.

● EAT LESS – Fatty meats and high fat products such as meat pâtés, pies and sausages.

● TRY INSTEAD – Low fat meats, such as chicken, turkey and venison.

Use only the leanest cuts of such meats as lamb, beef and pork.

Always cut any visible fat and skin from meat before cooking.

Choose reduced fat sausages and meat products and eat fish more often.

Try using low fat protein products such as Quorn or tofu in place of meat in recipes.

Make gravies using vegetable water or fat-free stock rather than using meat juices.

● EAT LESS – Full fat dairy products such as whole milk, cream, butter, hard margarine, crème fraîche, whole milk yogurts and hard cheese.

● TRY INSTEAD – Semi-skimmed or skimmed milk and milk products, low fat yogurts, low fat fromage frais and low fat soft cheeses, reduced fat hard cheeses such as Cheddar, and reduced fat creams and crème fraîche.

● EAT LESS – Hard cooking fats, such as lard or hard margarine.

● TRY INSTEAD – Polyunsaturated or monounsaturated oils, such as olive, sunflower or corn for cooking.

● EAT LESS – Rich salad dressings like full-fat mayonnaise, salad cream or French dressing.

● TRY INSTEAD – Reduced fat or fat-free mayonnaise or dressings. Make salad dressings at home with low fat yogurt or fromage frais.

● EAT LESS – Fried foods.

● TRY INSTEAD – Fat-free cooking methods such as grilling, microwaving, steaming or baking whenever possible.

Try cooking in a non-stick wok with only a very small amount of oil.

Always roast or grill meat or poultry on a rack.

● EAT LESS – Deep-fried chips and sautéed potatoes.

● TRY INSTEAD – Fat-free starchy foods such as pasta, couscous and rice.

Choose baked or boiled potatoes.

● EAT LESS – Added fat in cooking.

● TRY INSTEAD – To cook with little or no fat. Use heavy-based or good quality non-stick pans, so that the food doesn't stick.

Try using a small amount of spray oil in cooking to control exactly how much fat you are using.

Use fat-free or low fat ingredients for cooking, such as fruit juice, low fat or fat-free stock, wine or even beer.

● EAT LESS – High fat snacks such as crisps, tortilla chips, fried snacks and pastries, chocolate cakes, muffins, doughnuts, sweet pastries and biscuits – especially chocolate ones!

● TRY INSTEAD – Low fat and fat-free fresh or dried fruits, breadsticks or vegetable sticks.

Make your own home-baked low fat cakes and bakes.

If you do buy ready-made cakes and biscuits, always choose low fat and reduced fat versions.

FAT-FREE COOKING METHODS

It's very easy to cook without fat – whenever possible, grill, bake, microwave or steam foods without the addition of fat, or try stir-frying without fat – use a little low fat or fat-free stock, wine or fruit juice instead.

● Choosing heavy-based or good quality cookware, you'll find that the amount of fat needed for cooking foods can be kept to an absolute minimum. When making casseroles or meat sauces such as bolognese, dry-fry the meat to brown it and then drain off all the excess fat before adding the other ingredients. If you do need a little fat for cooking, choose an oil which is high in unsaturates such as corn, sunflower, olive or rapeseed oil and always use as little as possible.

● When baking low fat cakes and bakes, use good quality bakeware which doesn't need greasing before use, or use non-stick baking paper and only lightly grease before lining.

● Look out for non-stick coated fabric sheet. This re-usable non-stick material is amazingly versatile, it can be cut to size and used to line cake tins, baking sheets or frying pans. Heat resistant up to 290°C/550°F and microwave safe, it will last for up to 5 years.

● When baking foods such as chicken or fish, rather than adding a knob of butter to the food, try baking the food in a loosely sealed parcel of foil or greaseproof paper and adding some wine or fruit juice and herbs or spices to the food before sealing the parcel.

● When grilling foods, the addition of fat is often unnecessary. If the food shows signs of drying, lightly brush with a small amount of unsaturated oil such as sunflower or corn oil.

Above: Invest in a few of these useful items of cookware for easy fat-free cooking: non-stick cookware and accurate measuring equipment are essential.

● Microwaved foods rarely need the addition of fat, so add herbs or spices for extra flavour and colour.

● Steaming or boiling are easy, fat-free ways of cooking many foods, especially vegetables, fish and chicken.

● Try poaching foods, such as chicken, fish and fruit, in stock or syrup – it is another easy, fat-free cooking method.

● Try braising vegetables in the oven in low fat or fat-free stock, wine or simply water with the addition of some herbs.

● Sauté vegetables in low fat or fat-free stock, wine or fruit juice instead of fat or oil.

● Cook vegetables in a covered saucepan over a low heat with a little water so they cook in their own juices.

● Marinate food such as meat or poultry in mixtures of alcohol, herbs or spices, and vinegar or fruit juice. This will help to tenderize the meat and add flavour and colour and, in addition, the marinade can be used to baste the food while it is cooking.

● When serving vegetables such as boiled potatoes, carrots or peas, resist the temptation to add a knob of butter or margarine. Instead, sprinkle with chopped fresh herbs or ground spices.

COOKING WITH LOW FAT OR NON-FAT INGREDIENTS

Nowadays many foods are available in full fat and reduced fat or very low fat forms. In every supermarket you'll find a huge array of low fat dairy products, such as milk, cream, yogurt, hard and soft cheeses and fromage frais; reduced fat sweet or chocolate biscuits; reduced fat or fat-free salad dressings and mayonnaise; reduced fat crisps and snacks; low fat, half-fat or very low fat spreads; as well as such reduced fat ready-made food products as desserts.

Other foods, such as fresh fruit and vegetables, pasta, rice, potatoes and bread, naturally contain very little fat. Some foods, such as soy sauce, wine, cider, sherry, sugar, honey, syrup and jam, contain no fat at all. By combining these and other low fat foods you can create delicious dishes which contain very little fat.

Some low fat or reduced fat ingredients and products work better than others in cooking but often a simple substitution of one for another will work. The addition of low fat or non-fat ingredients, such as herbs and spices, also add plenty of extra flavour and colour to recipes.

LOW FAT SPREADS IN COOKING

There is a huge variety of low fat, reduced fat and half-fat spreads available in our supermarkets, along with some spreads that are very low in fat. Some are suitable for cooking, while others are only suitable for spreading.

Generally speaking, the very low fat spreads with a fat content of around 20% or less have a high water content and so are all unsuitable for cooking and are only suitable for spreading.

Low fat or half-fat spreads with a fat content of around 40% are suitable for spreading and can be used for some cooking methods. They are suitable for recipes such as all-in-one cake and biscuit recipes, all-in-one sauce recipes, sautéing vegetables over a low heat, choux pastry and some cake icings.

When using these low fat spreads for cooking, the fat may behave slightly differently to full fat products such as butter or margarine.

With some recipes, the cooked result may be slightly different, but will still be very acceptable. Other recipes will be just as tasty and successful. For example, choux pastry made using half- or low fat spread is often slightly crisper and lighter in texture than traditional choux pastry, and a cheesecake biscuit base made with melted half- or

low fat spread combined with crushed biscuit crumbs, may be slightly softer in texture and less crispy than a biscuit base made using melted butter.

When heating half- or low fat spreads, never cook them over a high heat. Always use a heavy-based pan over a low heat to avoid the product burning, spitting or spoiling, and stir all the time. With all-in-one sauces, the mixture should be whisked continuously over a low heat.

Half-fat or low fat spreads are not suitable for shallow or deep-fat frying, pastry making, rich fruit cakes, some biscuits, shortbread, clarified butter and preserves such as lemon curd.

Remember that the keeping qualities of recipes made using half- or low fat spreads may be reduced slightly, due to the lower fat content.

Almost all dairy products now come in low fat or reduced fat versions.

Another way to reduce the fat content of recipes, particularly cake recipes is to use a fruit purée in place of all or some of the fat in a recipe.

Many cake recipes work well using this method but others may not be so successful. Pastry does not work well. Breads work very well, perhaps because the amount of fat is usually relatively small, as do some biscuits and bars, such as brownies and flapjacks.

To make the dried fruit purée to use in recipes, chop 115g/4oz ready-to-eat dried fruit and place in a blender or food processor with 75ml/5 tbsp water and blend to a roughly smooth purée. Then, simply substitute the same weight of this dried fruit purée for all or just some of the amount of fat in the recipe. The purée will keep in the fridge for up to three days.

You can use prunes, dried apricots, dried peaches, or dried apples, or substitute mashed fresh fruit, such as ripe bananas or lightly cooked apples, without the added water.

Above: A selection of cooking oils and low fat spreads. Always check the packaging of low fat spreads – for cooking, they must have a fat content of about 40%.

LOW FAT AND VERY LOW FAT SNACKS

Instead of reaching for a packet of crisps, a high fat biscuit or a chocolate bar when hunger strikes, choose one of these tasty low fat snacks to fill that hungry hole.

● A piece of fresh fruit or vegetable such as an apple, banana or carrot – keep chunks or sticks wrapped in a polythene bag in the fridge.

● Fresh fruit or vegetable chunks – skewer them on to cocktail sticks or short bamboo skewers to make them into mini kebabs.

● A handful of dried fruit such as raisins, apricots or sultanas. These also make a perfect addition to children's packed lunches or to school break snacks.

● A portion of canned fruit in natural fruit juice – serve with a spoonful or two of fat-free yogurt.

● One or two crisp rice cakes – delicious on their own, or topped with honey, or reduced fat cheese.

● Crackers, such as water biscuits or crisp breads, spread with reduced sugar jam or marmalade.

● A bowl of wholewheat breakfast cereal or no-added-sugar muesli served with a little skimmed milk.

● Very low fat plain or fruit yogurt or fromage frais.

● A toasted teacake spread with reduced sugar jam or marmalade.

● Toasted crumpet spread with yeast extract or beef extract.

THE FAT AND CALORIE CONTENTS OF FOOD

The following figures show the weight of fat (g) and the energy content per 100g/4oz of each food.

VEGETABLES

	FAT (g)	ENERGY		FAT (g)	ENERGY
Broccoli	0.9	33 Kcals/138 kJ	Onions	0.2	36 Kcals/151 kJ
Cabbage	0.4	26 Kcals/109 kJ	Peas	1.5	83 Kcals/344 kJ
Carrots	0.3	35 Kcals/146 kJ	Potatoes	0.2	75 Kcals/318 kJ
Cauliflower	0.9	34 Kcals/142 kJ	Chips, home-made	6.7	189 Kcals/796 kJ
Courgettes	0.4	18 Kcals/74 kJ	Chips, retail	12.4	239 Kcals/1001 kJ
Cucumber	0.1	10 Kcals/40 kJ	Oven-chips, frozen, baked	4.2	162 Kcals/687 kJ
Mushrooms	0.5	13 Kcals/55 kJ	Tomatoes	0.3	17 Kcals/73 kJ

BEANS AND PULSES

	FAT (g)	ENERGY		FAT (g)	ENERGY
Black-eyed beans, cooked	1.8	116 Kcals/494 kJ	Hummus	12.6	187 Kcals/781 kJ
Butter beans, canned	0.5	77 Kcals/327 kJ	Red kidney beans, canned	0.6	100 Kcals/424 kJ
Chick-peas, canned	2.9	115 Kcals/487 kJ	Red lentils, cooked	0.4	100 Kcals/424 kJ

FISH AND SEAFOOD

	FAT (g)	ENERGY		FAT (g)	ENERGY
Cod fillets, raw	0.7	80 Kcals/337 kJ	Prawns	0.9	99 Kcals/418 kJ
Crab, canned	0.5	77 Kcals/326 kJ	Trout, grilled	5.4	135 Kcals/565 kJ
Haddock, raw	0.6	81 Kcals/345 kJ	Tuna, canned in brine	0.6	99 Kcals/422 kJ
Lemon sole, raw	1.5	83 Kcals/351 kJ	Tuna, canned in oil	9.0	189 Kcals/794 kJ

MEAT PRODUCTS

	FAT (g)	ENERGY		FAT (g)	ENERGY
Bacon rasher, streaky	39.5	414 Kcals/1710 kJ	Chicken fillet, raw	1.1	106 Kcals/449 kJ
Turkey rasher	1.0	99 Kcals/414 kJ	Chicken, roasted	12.5	218 Kcals/910 kJ
Beef mince, raw	16.2	225 Kcals/934 kJ	Duck, meat only, raw	6.5	137 Kcals/575 kJ
Beef mince, extra lean, raw	9.6	174 Kcals/728 kJ	Duck, roasted, meat,		
Rump steak, lean and fat	10.1	174 Kcals/726 kJ	fat and skin	38.1	423 Kcals/1750 kJ
Rump steak, lean only	4.1	125 Kcals/526 kJ	Turkey, meat only, raw	1.6	105 Kcals/443 kJ
Lamb chops, loin, lean and fat	23.0	277 Kcals/1150 kJ	Liver, lamb, raw	6.2	137 Kcals/575 kJ
Lamb, average, lean, raw	8.3	156 Kcals/651 kJ	Pork pie	27.0	376 Kcals/1564 kJ
Pork chops, loin, lean and fat	21.7	270 Kcals/1119 kJ	Salami	45.2	491 Kcals/2031 kJ
Pork, average, lean, raw	4.0	123 Kcals/519 kJ	Sausage roll, flaky pastry	36.4	477 Kcals/1985 kJ

Information from *The Composition of Foods* (5th Edition 1991) is reproduced with the permission of the Royal Society of Chemistry and the Controller of Her Majesty's Stationery Office.

DAIRY, FATS AND OILS

	FAT (g)	ENERGY		FAT (g)	ENERGY
Cream, double	48.0	449 Kcals/1849 kJ	Low fat yogurt, plain	0.8	56 Kcals/236 kJ
Cream, single	19.1	198 Kcals/817 kJ	Greek yogurt	9.1	115 Kcals/477 kJ
Cream, whipping	39.3	373 Kcals/1539 kJ	Reduced fat Greek yogurt	5.0	80 Kcals/335 kJ
Crème fraîche	40.0	379 Kcals/156 kJ	Butter	81.7	737 Kcals/3031 kJ
Reduced fat crème fraîche	15.0	165 Kcals/683 kJ	Margarine	81.6	739 Kcals/3039 kJ
Reduced fat double cream	24.0	243 Kcals/1002 kJ	Low fat spread	40.5	390 Kcals/1605 kJ
Milk, skimmed	0.1	33 Kcals/130 kJ	Very low fat spread	25	273 Kcals/1128 kJ
Milk, whole	3.9	66 Kcals/275 kJ	Lard	99.0	891 Kcals/3663 kJ
Brie	26.9	319 Kcals/1323 kJ	Corn oil	99.9	899 Kcals/3696 kJ
Cheddar cheese	34.4	412 Kcals/1708 kJ	Olive oil	99.9	899 Kcals/3696 kJ
Cheddar-type, reduced fat	15.0	261 Kcals/1091 kJ	Safflower oil	99.9	899 Kcals/3696 kJ
Cream cheese	47.4	439 Kcals/1807 kJ	Eggs	10.8	147 Kcals/612 kJ
Fromage frais, plain	7.1	113 Kcals/469 kJ	Egg yolk	30.5	339 Kcals/1402 kJ
Fromage frais, very low fat	0.2	58 Kcals/247 kJ	Egg white	Trace	36 Kcals/153 kJ
Skimmed milk soft cheese	Trace	74 Kcals/313 kJ	Fat-free dressing	1.2	67 Kcals/282 kJ
Edam cheese	25.4	333 Kcals/1382 kJ	French dressing	49.4	462 Kcals/1902 kJ
Feta cheese	20.2	250 Kcals/1037 kJ	Mayonnaise	75.6	691 Kcals2843 kJ
Parmesan cheese	32.7	452 Kcals/1880 kJ	Mayonnaise, reduced calorie	28.1	288 Kcals/1188 kJ

CEREALS, BAKING AND PRESERVES

	FAT (g)	ENERGY		FAT (g)	ENERGY
Brown rice, uncooked	2.8	357 Kcals/1518 kJ	Digestive biscuit (plain)	20.9	471 Kcals/1978 kJ
White rice, uncooked	3.6	383 Kcals/1630 kJ	Reduced fat digestive biscuits	16.4	467 Kcals/1965 kJ
Pasta, white, uncooked	1.8	342 Kcals/1456 kJ	Shortbread	26.1	498 Kcals/2087 kJ
Pasta, wholemeal, uncooked	2.5	324 Kcal/1379 kJ	Madeira cake	16.9	393 Kcals/1652 kJ
Brown bread	2.0	218 Kcals/927 kJ	Fatless sponge cake	6.1	294 Kcals/1245 kJ
White bread	1.9	235 Kcals/1002 kJ	Doughnut, jam	14.5	336 Kcals/1414 kJ
Wholemeal bread	2.5	215 Kcals914 kJ	Sugar, white	0 3	94 Kcals/1680 kJ
Cornflakes	0.7	360 Kcals/1535 kJ	Chocolate, milk	30.7	520 Kcals/2177 kJ
Sultana bran	1.6	303 Kcals/1289 kJ	Chocolate, plain	28	510 Kcals/2157 kJ
Swiss-style muesli	5.9	363 Kcals/1540 kJ	Honey	0	288 Kcals/1229 kJ
Croissant	20.3	360 Kcals/1505 kJ	Lemon curd	5.0	283 Kcals/1198 kJ
Flapjack	26.6	484 Kcals/2028 kJ	Fruit jam	0 26	268 Kcals/1114 kJ

FRUIT AND NUTS

	FAT (g)	ENERGY		FAT (g)	ENERGY
Apples, eating	0.1	47 Kcals/199 kJ	Pears	0.1	40 Kcals/169 kJ
Avocados	19.5	190 Kcals/784 kJ	Almonds	55.8	612 Kcals/2534 kJ
Bananas	0.3	95 Kcals/403 kJ	Brazil nuts	68.2	682 Kcals/2813 kJ
Dried mixed fruit	0.4	268 Kcals/1114 kJ	Hazelnuts	63.5	650 Kcals/2685 kJ
Grapefruit	0.1	30 Kcals/126 kJ	Pine nuts	68.6	688 Kcals/2840 kJ
Oranges	0.1	37 Kcals/158 kJ	Walnuts	68.5	688 Kcals/2837kJ
Peaches	0.1	33 Kcals/142 kJ	Peanut butter, smooth	53.7	623 Kcals/2581 kJ

SOUPS

Home-made soups are ideal served as a starter, a snack or a light lunch. They are filling, nutritious and low in fat and are delicious served with a chunk of fresh crusty bread. The wide variety of fresh vegetables available nowadays ensures that the freshest ingredients can be used to create tempting and delicious home-made soups. We include a tasty selection, including vegetable soups, chowders and bean and pasta soups. Choose from temptations such as Italian Vegetable Soup, Spicy Tomato and Lentil Soup, and Creamy Cod Chowder.

ITALIAN VEGETABLE SOUP

The success of this clear soup depends on the quality of the stock, so for the best results, be sure you use home-made vegetable stock rather than stock cubes.

INGREDIENTS

Serves 4

1 small carrot
1 baby leek
1 celery stick
50g/2oz green cabbage
900ml/1½ pints/3¾ cups vegetable stock
1 bay leaf
115g/4oz/1 cup cooked cannellini or haricot beans
25g/1oz/⅕ cup soup pasta, such as tiny shells, bows, stars or elbows
salt and black pepper
snipped fresh chives, to garnish

1 Cut the carrot, leek and celery into 5cm/2in long julienne strips. Slice the cabbage very finely.

NUTRITION NOTES

Per portion:

Energy	69Kcals/288kJ
Protein	3.67g
Fat	0.71g
Saturated Fat	0.05g
Fibre	2.82g

2 Put the stock and bay leaf into a large saucepan and bring to the boil. Add the carrot, leek and celery, cover and simmer for 6 minutes.

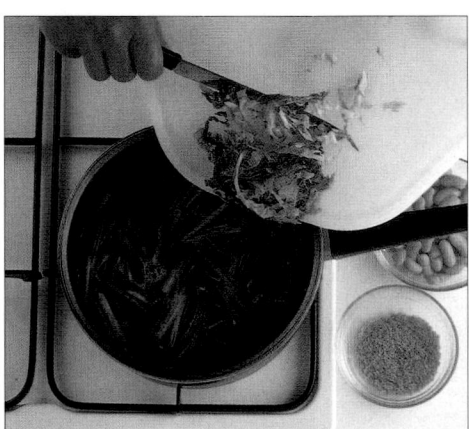

3 Add the cabbage, beans and pasta shapes. Stir, then simmer uncovered for a further 4–5 minutes, or until the vegetables and pasta are tender.

4 Remove the bay leaf and season with salt and pepper to taste. Ladle into four soup bowls and garnish with snipped chives. Serve immediately.

CHICKEN AND PASTA SOUP

INGREDIENTS

Serves 4–6

900ml/1½ pints/3¾ cups chicken stock
1 bay leaf
4 spring onions, sliced
225g/8oz button mushrooms, sliced
115g/4oz cooked chicken breast
50g/2oz soup pasta
150ml/¼ pint/⅔ cup dry white wine
15ml/1 tbsp chopped fresh parsley
salt and black pepper

NUTRITION NOTES

Per portion:

Energy	126Kcals/529kJ
Fat	2.2g
Saturated Fat	0.6g
Cholesterol	19mg
Fibre	1.3g

1 Put the stock and bay leaf into a pan and bring to the boil.

2 Add the spring onions and mushrooms to the stock.

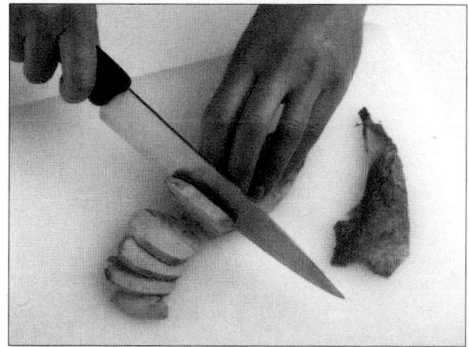

3 Remove the skin from the chicken and slice the meat thinly using a sharp knife. Add to the soup and season to taste. Heat through for about 2–3 minutes.

4 Add the pasta, cover and simmer for 7–8 minutes. Just before serving, add the wine and chopped parsley, heat through for 2–3 minutes, then season to taste.

BEETROOT SOUP WITH RAVIOLI

INGREDIENTS

Serves 4–6

1 quantity basic pasta dough (see
   page 68)
egg white, beaten, for brushing
flour, for dusting
1 small onion or shallot, finely chopped
2 garlic cloves, crushed
5ml/1 tsp fennel seeds
600ml/1 pint/2½ cups chicken stock
225g/8oz cooked beetroot
30ml/2 tbsp fresh orange juice
fennel or dill leaves, to garnish
crusty bread, to serve

For the filling

115g/4oz mushrooms, finely chopped
1 shallot or small onion, finely chopped
1–2 garlic cloves, crushed
5ml/1 tsp chopped fresh thyme
15ml/1 tbsp chopped fresh parsley
90ml/6 tbsp fresh white breadcrumbs
salt and black pepper
large pinch of ground nutmeg

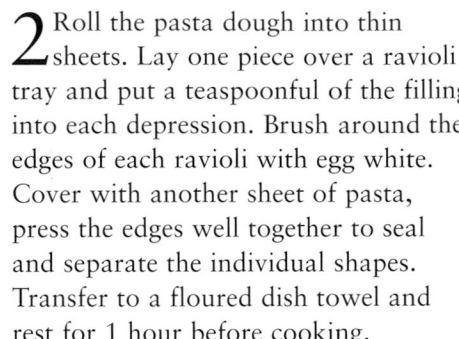

1 Process all the filling ingredients and
scoop into a bowl.

NUTRITION NOTES

Per portion:	
Energy	358Kcals/1504kJ
Fat	4.9g
Saturated Fat	1.0g
Cholesterol	110mg
Fibre	4.3g

2 Roll the pasta dough into thin
sheets. Lay one piece over a ravioli
tray and put a teaspoonful of the filling
into each depression. Brush around the
edges of each ravioli with egg white.
Cover with another sheet of pasta,
press the edges well together to seal
and separate the individual shapes.
Transfer to a floured dish towel and
rest for 1 hour before cooking.

3 Cook the ravioli in a large pan of
boiling, salted water for 2 minutes,
in batches to stop them sticking together. Remove and drop into a bowl of
cold water for 5 seconds before placing
on a tray. (You can make these pasta
shapes a day in advance. Cover with
clear film and store in the fridge.)

4 Put the onion, garlic and fennel
seeds into a pan with 150ml/
¼ pint/⅔ cup of the stock. Bring to the
boil, cover and simmer for 5 minutes
until tender. Peel and finely dice the
beetroot (reserve 60ml/4 tbsp for the
garnish). Add the rest of the beetroot to
the soup with the remaining stock and
bring to the boil.

5 Add the orange juice and cooked
ravioli and simmer for 2 minutes.
Pour into shallow soup bowls and
garnish with the reserved diced
beetroot and fennel or dill leaves.

Spicy Tomato and Lentil Soup

INGREDIENTS

Serves 4

15ml/1 tbsp sunflower oil
1 onion, finely chopped
1–2 garlic cloves, crushed
2.5cm/1in piece fresh root ginger,
   peeled and finely chopped
5ml/1 tsp cumin seeds, crushed
450g/1lb ripe tomatoes, peeled, seeded
   and chopped
115g/4oz/½ cup red split lentils
1.2 litres/2 pints/5 cups vegetable or
   chicken stock
15ml/1 tbsp tomato purée
salt and black pepper
low fat natural yogurt and chopped
   fresh parsley, to garnish (optional)

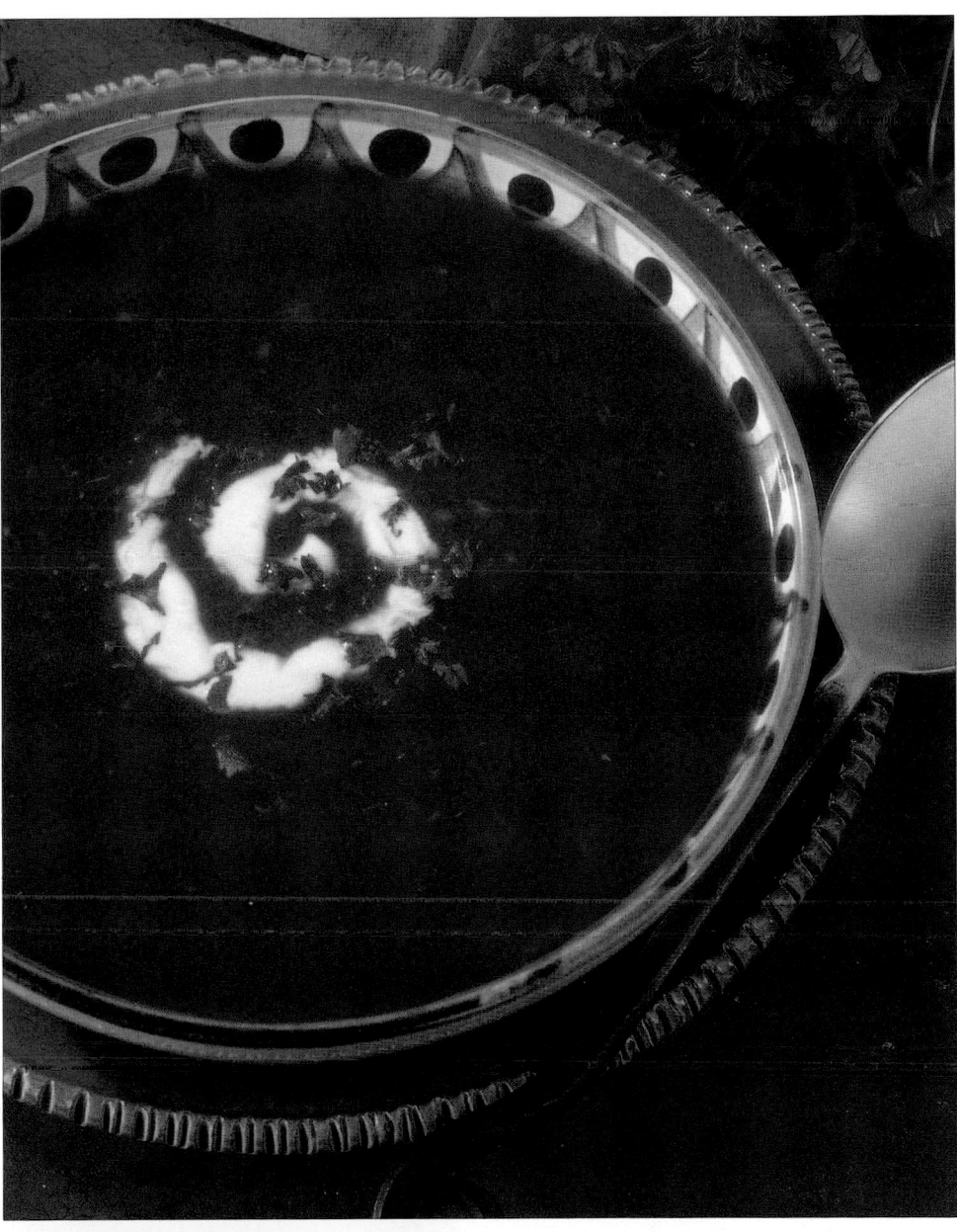

1 Heat the sunflower oil in a large
heavy-based saucepan and cook the
chopped onion gently for 5 minutes
until softened.

2 Stir in the garlic, ginger and cumin,
followed by the tomatoes and
lentils. Cook over a low heat for a
further 3–4 minutes.

3 Stir in the stock and tomato purée.
Bring to the boil, then lower the
heat and simmer gently for about
30 minutes until the lentils are soft.
Season to taste with salt and pepper.

4 Purée the soup in a blender or food
processor. Return to the clean pan
and reheat gently. Serve in heated
bowls. If liked, garnish each portion
with a swirl of yogurt and a little
chopped parsley.

NUTRITION NOTES	
Per portion:	
Energy	165Kcals/695kJ
Fat	4g
Saturated Fat	0.5g
Cholesterol	0

CREAMY COD CHOWDER

A delicious light version of a classic, this chowder is a tasty combination of smoked fish, vegetables, fresh herbs and milk. To cut the calories and stock even more, use vegetable or fish stock in place of the milk. Serve as a substantial starter or snack, or as a light main meal accompanied by warm crusty wholemeal bread.

INGREDIENTS

Serves 4–6
350g/12oz smoked cod fillet
1 small onion, finely chopped
1 bay leaf
4 black peppercorns
900ml/1½ pints/3¾ cups skimmed milk
10ml/2 tsp cornflour
200g/7oz canned sweetcorn kernels
15ml/1 tbsp chopped fresh parsley

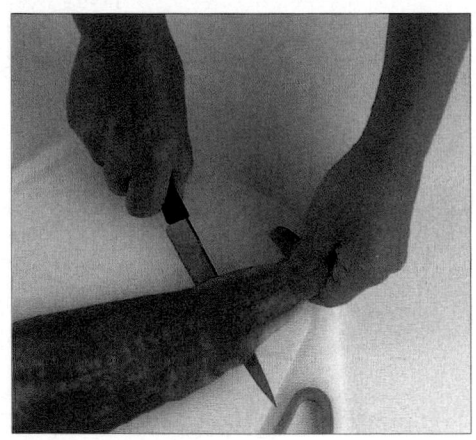

1 Skin the fish and put it into a large saucepan with the onion, bay leaf and peppercorns. Pour over the milk.

2 Bring to the boil, then reduce the heat and simmer very gently for 12–15 minutes, or until the fish is just cooked. Do not overcook.

3 Using a slotted spoon, lift out the fish and flake into large chunks. Remove the bay leaf and peppercorns and discard.

4 Blend the cornflour with 10ml/2 tsp cold water and add to the saucepan. Bring to the boil and simmer for about 1 minute or until slightly thickened.

5 Drain the sweetcorn kernels and add to the saucepan together with the flaked fish and parsley. Reheat gently and serve.

COOK'S TIP
The flavour of the chowder improves if it is made a day in advance. Leave to cool, then chill in the fridge until required. Reheat gently. Do not allow the soup to boil, or the fish will disintegrate.

NUTRITION NOTES

Per portion:	
Energy	200Kcals/840kJ
Protein	24.71g
Fat	1.23g
Saturated Fat	0.32g

SPINACH AND BEAN CURD SOUP

This appetizing clear soup has an extremely delicate and mild flavour that can be used as a perfect counterbalance to the intense heat of a hot Thai curry.

INGREDIENTS

Serves 6

30ml/2 tbsp dried shrimps
1 litre/1¾ pints/4 cups chicken stock
225g/8oz fresh bean curd, drained and
 cut into 2cm/¾in cubes
30ml/2 tbsp fish sauce
350g/12oz fresh spinach, washed
 thoroughly
black pepper
2 spring onions, finely sliced, to garnish

1 Rinse and drain the dried shrimps. Combine the shrimps with the chicken stock in a large saucepan and bring to the boil.

2 Add the bean curd and simmer for about 5 minutes. Season with fish sauce and black pepper to taste.

3 Tear the spinach leaves into bite-size pieces and add to the soup. Cook for another 1–2 minutes.

4 Remove from the heat and sprinkle with the finely sliced spring onions, to garnish.

NUTRITION NOTES

Per portion:

Energy	64Kcals/270kJ
Fat	225g
Saturated Fat	0.26g
Cholesterol	25mg
Fibre	1.28g

COOK'S TIP
Home-made chicken stock makes the world of difference to clear soups. Accumulate enough bones to make a big batch of stock, use what you need and keep the rest in the freezer.

Put 1.5kg/3–3½lb meaty chicken bones and 450g/1lb pork bones (optional) into a large saucepan. Add 3 litres/5 pints/12 cups water and slowly bring to the boil. Occasionally skim off and discard any scum that rises to the surface. Add 2 slices fresh root ginger, 2 garlic cloves (optional), 2 celery sticks, 4 spring onions, 2 bruised lemon grass stalks, a few sprigs of coriander and 10 crushed black peppercorns. Reduce the heat to low and simmer for about 2–2½ hours.

Remove from the heat and leave to cool, uncovered and undisturbed. Pour through a fine strainer, leaving the last dregs behind as they tend to cloud the soup. Leave to cool, then chill. Use as required, removing any fat that congeals on the surface.

VEGETABLE MINESTRONE

INGREDIENTS

Serves 6–8
large pinch of saffron strands
1 onion, chopped
1 leek, sliced
1 stick celery, sliced
2 carrots, diced
2–3 garlic cloves, crushed
600ml/1 pint/2½ cups chicken stock
2 x 400g/14oz cans chopped tomatoes
50g/2oz/½ cup frozen peas
50g/2oz soup pasta (anellini)
5ml/1 tsp caster sugar
15ml/1 tbsp chopped fresh parsley
15ml/1 tbsp chopped fresh basil
salt and black pepper

1 Soak the pinch of saffron strands in 15ml/1 tbsp boiling water. Leave to stand for 10 minutes.

2 Meanwhile, put the prepared onion, leek, celery, carrots and garlic into a large pan. Add the chicken stock, bring to the boil, cover and simmer for about 10 minutes.

3 Add the canned tomatoes, the saffron with its liquid and the frozen peas. Bring back to the boil and add the soup pasta. Simmer for 10 minutes until tender.

> **COOK'S TIP**
> Saffron strands aren't essential for this soup, but they give a wonderful delicate flavour, with the bonus of a lovely rich orange-yellow colour.

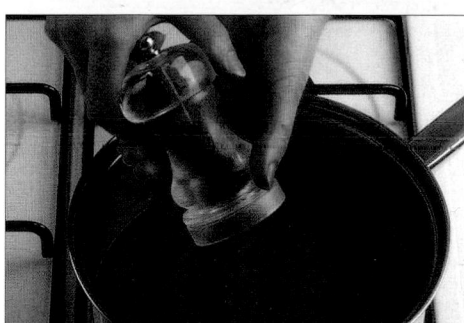

4 Season with sugar, salt and pepper to taste. Stir in the chopped herbs just before serving.

NUTRITION NOTES	
Per portion:	
Energy	87Kcals/367kJ
Fat	0.7g
Saturated Fat	0.1g
Cholesterol	0
Fibre	3.3g

SWEETCORN CHOWDER WITH PASTA SHELLS

Smoked turkey rashers provide a tasty, low fat alternative to bacon in this hearty dish. If you prefer, omit the meat altogether and serve the soup as is.

INGREDIENTS

Serves 4

1 small green pepper
450g/1lb potatoes, peeled and diced
350g/12oz/2 cups canned or frozen
  sweetcorn
1 onion, chopped
1 celery stick, chopped
a bouquet garni (bay leaf, parsley stalks
  and thyme)
600ml/1 pint/2½ cups chicken stock
300ml/½ pint/1¼ cups skimmed milk
50g/2oz small pasta shells
oil, for frying
150g/5oz smoked turkey rashers, diced
salt and black pepper
bread sticks, to serve

1 Halve the green pepper, then remove the stalk and seeds. Cut the flesh into small dice, cover with boiling water and stand for 2 minutes. Drain and rinse.

NUTRITION NOTES

Per portion:

Energy	215Kcals/904kJ
Fat	1.6g
Saturated Fat	0.3g
Cholesterol	13mg
Fibre	2.8g

2 Put the potatoes into a saucepan with the sweetcorn, onion, celery, green pepper, bouquet garni and stock. Bring to the boil, cover and simmer for 20 minutes until tender.

3 Add the milk and season with salt and pepper. Process half of the soup in a food processor or blender and return to the pan with the pasta shells. Simmer for 10 minutes.

4 Fry the turkey rashers in a non-stick frying pan for 2–3 minutes. Stir into the soup. Season to taste and serve with bread sticks.

CARROT AND CORIANDER SOUP

Nearly all root vegetables make excellent soups as they purée well and have an earthy flavour which complements the sharper flavours of herbs and spices. Carrots are particularly versatile, and this simple soup is elegant in both flavour and appearance.

INGREDIENTS

Serves 6

10ml/2 tsp sunflower oil
1 onion, chopped
1 celery stick, sliced, plus 2–3 leafy
  celery tops
2 small potatoes, chopped
450g/1lb carrots, preferably young and
  tender, chopped
1 litre/1¾ pints/4 cups chicken stock
10–15ml/2–3 tsp ground coriander
15ml/1 tbsp chopped fresh coriander
200ml/7fl oz/1 cup semi-skimmed milk
salt and black pepper

1 Heat the oil in a large flameproof casserole or heavy-based saucepan and fry the onion over a gentle heat for 3–4 minutes until slightly softened but not browned. Add the celery and potato, cook for a few minutes, then add the carrot. Fry over a gentle heat for 3–4 minutes, stirring frequently, and then cover. Reduce the heat even further and cook for about 10 minutes. Shake the pan or stir occasionally so the vegetables do not stick to the base.

2 Add the stock, bring to the boil and then partially cover and simmer for a further 8–10 minutes until the carrot and potato are tender.

3 Remove 6–8 tiny celery leaves for a garnish and finely chop about 15ml/1 tbsp of the remaining celery tops. In a small saucepan, dry fry the ground coriander for about 1 minute, stirring constantly. Reduce the heat, add the chopped celery and fresh coriander and fry for about 1 minute. Set aside.

4 Process the soup in a food processor or blender and pour into a clean saucepan. Stir in the milk, coriander mixture and seasoning. Heat gently, taste and adjust the seasoning. Serve garnished with the reserved celery.

NUTRITION NOTES	
Per portion:	
Energy	76.5Kcals/320kJ
Fat	3.2g
Saturated fat	0.65g
Cholesterol	2.3mg
Fibre	2.2g

COOK'S TIP
For a more piquant flavour, add a little freshly squeezed lemon juice just before serving. The contrast between the orange-coloured soup and the green garnish is a feast for the eye as well as the tastebuds.

CHICKEN AND COCONUT SOUP

This aromatic soup is rich with coconut milk and intensely flavoured with galangal, lemon grass and kaffir lime leaves.

INGREDIENTS

Serves 4–6

750ml/1¼ pints/3 cups coconut milk
475ml/16fl oz/2 cups chicken stock
4 lemon grass stalks, bruised and
    chopped
2.5cm/1in section galangal, thinly sliced
10 black peppercorns, crushed
10 kaffir lime leaves, torn
300g/11oz boneless chicken, cut into
    thin strips
115g/4oz button mushrooms
50g/2oz baby sweetcorn
60ml/4 tbsp lime juice
about 45ml/3 tbsp fish sauce
2 fresh chillies, seeded and chopped,
    chopped spring onions, and coriander
    leaves, to garnish

1 Bring the coconut milk and chicken stock to the boil. Add the lemon grass, galangal, peppercorns and half the kaffir lime leaves. Reduce the heat and simmer gently for 10 minutes.

2 Strain the stock into a clean pan. Return to the heat, then add the chicken, button mushrooms and baby sweetcorn. Simmer for 5–7 minutes or until the chicken is cooked.

3 Stir in the lime juice, fish sauce to taste and the rest of the lime leaves. Serve hot, garnished with chillies, spring onions and coriander.

NUTRITION NOTES

Per portion:

Energy	144Kcals/609kJ
Fat	2.5g
Saturated Fat	0.55g
Cholesterol	67.5mg
Fibre	0.6g

HOT AND SOUR PRAWN SOUP

This is a classic Thai seafood soup and is probably the most popular and well known soup from Thailand.

INGREDIENTS

Serves 4–6

450g/1lb king prawns
1 litre/1¾ pints/4 cups chicken stock
3 lemon grass stalks
10 kaffir lime leaves, torn in half
225g/8oz can straw mushrooms,
    drained
45ml/3 tbsp fish sauce
50ml/2fl oz/¼ cup lime juice
30ml/2 tbsp chopped spring onions
15ml/1 tbsp coriander leaves
4 fresh chillies, seeded and chopped
salt and black pepper

1 Shell and devein the prawns and set aside. Rinse the prawn shells, place them in a large saucepan with the stock and bring to the boil.

2 Bruise the lemon grass stalks with the blunt edge of a chopping knife and add them to the stock together with half the lime leaves. Simmer gently for 5–6 minutes, until the stalks change colour and the stock is fragrant.

NUTRITION NOTES

Per portion:

Energy	49Kcals/209kJ
Fat	0.45g
Saturated Fat	0.07g
Cholesterol	78.8mg
Fibre	0.09g

3 Strain the stock, return to the saucepan and reheat. Add the mushrooms and prawns, then cook until the prawns turn pink. Stir in the fish sauce, lime juice, spring onions, coriander, chillies and the rest of the lime leaves. Taste the soup and adjust the seasoning – it should be sour, salty, spicy and hot.

RED ONION AND BEETROOT SOUP

This beautiful vivid ruby-red soup will look stunning at any dinner party.

INGREDIENTS

Serves 6
10ml/2 tsp olive oil
350g/12oz red onions, sliced
2 garlic cloves, crushed
275g/10oz cooked beetroot, cut into
   sticks
1.2 litres/2 pints/5 cups vegetable stock
   or water
50g/2oz/1 cup cooked soup pasta
30ml/2 tbsp raspberry vinegar
salt and black pepper
low fat yogurt and snipped chives,
   to garnish

COOK'S TIP
If you prefer, try substituting cooked barley for the pasta to give extra nuttiness.

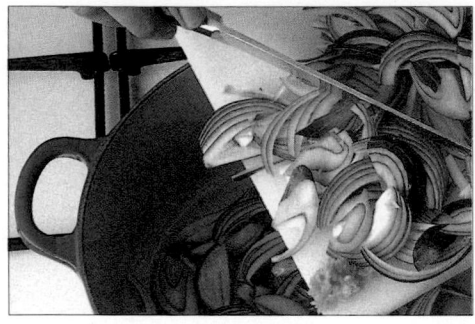

1 Heat the olive oil and add the onions and garlic.

2 Cook gently for about 20 minutes or until soft and tender.

3 Add the beetroot, stock or water, cooked pasta shapes and vinegar and heat through.

4 Adjust the seasoning to taste. Ladle the soup into bowls. Top each one with a spoonful of yogurt and sprinkle with snipped chives. Serve piping hot.

NUTRITION NOTES	
Per portion:	
Energy	76Kcals/318kJ
Fat	2.01g
Saturated Fat	0.28g
Cholesterol	0.33mg
Fibre	1.83g

CAULIFLOWER AND BEAN SOUP

The sweet, liquorice flavour of the fennel seeds gives a delicious edge to this hearty soup.

INGREDIENTS

Serves 6
10ml/2 tsp olive oil
1 garlic clove, crushed
1 onion, chopped
10ml/2 tsp fennel seeds
1 cauliflower, cut into small florets
2 x 400g/14oz cans flageolet beans,
  drained and rinsed
1.2 litres/2 pints/5 cups vegetable stock
  or water
salt and black pepper
chopped fresh parsley, to garnish
toasted slices of French bread, to serve

1 Heat the olive oil. Add the garlic, onion and fennel seeds and cook gently for 5 minutes or until the onion is softened.

2 Add the cauliflower, half of the beans and all the stock or water.

3 Bring to the boil. Reduce the heat and simmer for 10 minutes or until the cauliflower is tender.

NUTRITION NOTES	
Per portion:	
Energy	194.3Kcals/822.5kJ
Fat	3.41g
Saturated Fat	0.53g
Cholesterol	0
Fibre	7.85g

4 Pour the soup into a blender and blend until smooth. Stir in the remaining beans and season to taste. Reheat and pour into bowls. Sprinkle with chopped parsley and serve with toasted slices of French bread.

MELON AND BASIL SOUP

A deliciously refreshing, chilled fruit soup, just right for a hot summer's day. It takes next to no time to prepare, leaving you free to enjoy the sunshine and, even better, it is almost totally fat-free.

INGREDIENTS

Serves 4–6
2 Charentais or rock melons
75g/3oz/6 tbsp caster sugar
175ml/6fl oz/³/₄ cup water
finely grated rind and juice of 1 lime
45ml/3 tbsp shredded fresh basil
fresh basil leaves, to garnish

1 Cut the melons in half across the middle. Scrape out the seeds and discard. Using a melon baller, scoop out 20–24 balls and set aside for the garnish. Scoop out the remaining flesh and place in a blender or food processor. Set aside.

2 Place the sugar, water and lime zest in a small pan over a low heat. Stir until dissolved, bring to the boil and simmer for 2–3 minutes. Remove from the heat and leave to cool slightly. Pour half the mixture into the blender or food processor with the melon flesh. Blend until smooth, adding the remaining syrup and lime juice to taste.

3 Pour the mixture into a bowl, stir in the basil and chill. Serve garnished with basil leaves and melon balls.

NUTRITION NOTES

Per portion:

Energy	69Kcals/293.8kJ
Fat	0.14g
Saturated Fat	0
Cholesterol	0
Fibre	0.47g

COOK'S TIP
Add the syrup in two stages, as the amount of sugar needed will depend on the sweetness of the melon.

CHILLED FRESH TOMATO SOUP

This effortless uncooked soup can be made in minutes.

INGREDIENTS

Serves 6
1.5kg/3–3½lb ripe tomatoes, peeled and roughly chopped
4 garlic cloves, crushed
30ml/2 tbsp balsamic vinegar
4 thick slices wholemeal bread
black pepper
low fat fromage frais, to garnish

1 Place the tomatoes in a blender with the garlic. Blend until smooth.

2 Pass the mixture through a sieve to remove the seeds. Stir in balsamic vinegar and season to taste with pepper. Put in the fridge to chill.

3 Toast the bread lightly on both sides. While still hot, cut off the crusts and slice the toast in half horizontally. Place on a board with the uncooked sides facing down and, using a circular motion, rub to remove any doughy pieces of bread.

COOK'S TIP
For the best flavour, it is important to use only fully ripened, flavourful tomatoes in this soup.

NUTRITION NOTES	
Per portion:	
Energy	111Kcals/475kJ
Fat	1.42g
Saturated Fat	0.39g
Cholesterol	0.16mg
Fibre	4.16g

4 Cut each slice into four triangles. Place on a grill pan and toast the uncooked sides until lightly golden. Garnish each bowl of soup with a spoonful of fromage frais and serve with the Melba toast.

STARTERS AND SNACKS

Healthy low fat starters provide a delicious start to a meal and are quick and easy to make. Starters should not be too filling as they are simply setting the scene for the low fat main course to follow. Choose from a tempting selection of recipes, including light and refreshing fruit cocktails such as Minted Melon and Grapefruit and vegetable pâtés or dips such as Guacamole with Crudités. Quick and easy snacks and light dishes are ideal served with thick slices of warm, crusty bread for a low fat, nutritious lunch or supper. We include a selection of tasty snacks, such as Pasta with Herby Scallops, Cheese and Chutney Toasties and Parma Ham and Pepper Pizzas.

MELON, PINEAPPLE AND GRAPE COCKTAIL

A light, refreshing fruit salad, with no added sugar and virtually no fat, perfect for breakfast or brunch – or any time.

— INGREDIENTS —

Serves 4

½ melon
225g/8oz fresh pineapple or 225g/8oz
*   can pineapple chunks in own juice*
225g/8oz seedless white grapes, halved
120ml/4fl oz/½ cup white grape juice
fresh mint leaves, to decorate (optional)

1 Remove the seeds from the melon half and use a melon baller to scoop out even-size balls.

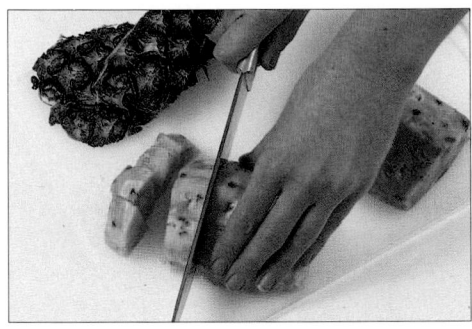

2 Using a sharp knife, cut the skin from the pineapple and discard. Cut the fruit into bite-size chunks.

3 Combine all the fruits in a glass serving dish and pour over the juice. If you are using canned pineapple, measure the drained juice and make it up to the required quantity with the grape juice.

4 If not serving immediately, cover and chill. Serve decorated with mint leaves, if liked.

NUTRITION NOTES

Per portion:

Energy	95Kcals/395kJ
Fat	0.5g
Saturated Fat	0
Cholesterol	0

GRAPEFRUIT SALAD WITH ORANGE

The bitter-sweet flavour of Campari combines especially well with citrus fruit. Because of its alcohol content, this dish is not suitable for young children.

INGREDIENTS

Serves 4

45ml/3 tbsp caster sugar
60ml/4 tbsp Campari
30ml/2 tbsp lemon juice
4 grapefruit
5 oranges
4 sprigs fresh mint

NUTRITION NOTES

Per portion:

Energy	196Kcals/822kJ
Fat	5.9g
Saturated Fat	2.21g
Cholesterol	66.37mg
Fibre	1.6g

1 Bring 150ml/5fl oz/²/₃ cup water to the boil in a small saucepan, add the sugar and simmer until dissolved. Leave to cool, then add the Campari and lemon juice. Chill until ready to serve.

COOK'S TIP
When buying citrus fruit, choose brightly coloured specimens that feel heavy for their size.

2 Cut the peel from the grapefruit and oranges with a serrated knife. Segment the fruit into a bowl by slipping a small paring knife between the flesh and the membranes. Combine the fruit with the Campari syrup and chill.

3 Spoon the salad into four dishes and garnish each dish with a sprig of fresh mint.

MINTED MELON AND GRAPEFRUIT

Melon is always a popular starter. Here the succulent flavour of the Galia melon is complemented by the refreshing taste of citrus fruit and a simple mustard and vinegar dressing. Fresh mint, used in the cocktail and as a garnish, enhances both its flavour and appearance.

INGREDIENTS

Serves 4

1 small Galia melon, weighing about
  1kg/2¼lb
2 pink grapefruit
1 yellow grapefruit
5ml/1 tsp Dijon mustard
5ml/1 tsp raspberry or sherry vinegar
5ml/1 tsp clear honey
15ml/1 tbsp chopped fresh mint
sprigs of fresh mint,
  to garnish

1 Halve the melon and remove the seeds with a teaspoon. With a melon baller, carefully scoop the flesh into balls.

NUTRITION NOTES	
Per portion:	
Energy	97Kcals/409kJ
Protein	2.22g
Fat	0.63g
Saturated Fat	0
Fibre	3.05g

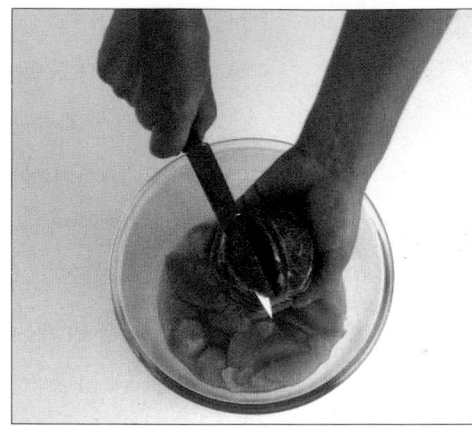

2 With a small sharp knife, peel the grapefruit and remove all the white pith. Remove the segments by cutting between the membranes, holding the fruit over a small bowl to catch any juices.

3 Whisk the mustard, vinegar, honey, chopped mint and grapefruit juices together in a mixing bowl. Add the melon balls together with the grapefruit and mix well. Chill for 30 minutes.

4 Ladle the fruit into four glass dishes and serve garnished with sprigs of fresh mint.

GUACAMOLE WITH CRUDITÉS

This fresh-tasting spicy dip is made using peas instead of the avocado pears that are traditionally associated with this dish. This version saves on both fat and calories, without compromising on taste.

INGREDIENTS

Serves 4–6
350g/12oz/2¼ cups frozen peas, defrosted
1 garlic clove, crushed
2 spring onions, chopped
5ml/1 tsp finely grated rind and juice of 1 lime
2.5ml/½ tsp ground cumin
dash of Tabasco sauce
15ml/1 tbsp reduced fat mayonnaise
30ml/2 tbsp chopped fresh coriander or parsley
salt and black pepper
pinch of paprika and lime slices, to garnish

For the crudités
6 baby carrots
2 celery sticks
1 red-skinned eating apple
1 pear
15ml/1 tbsp lemon or lime juice
6 baby sweetcorn

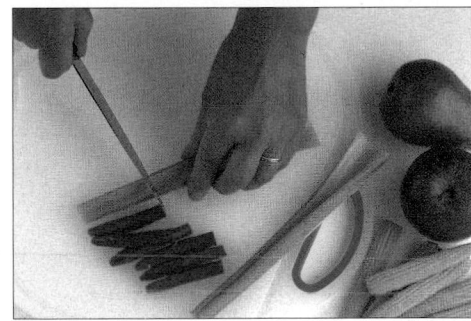

1 Put the peas, garlic clove, spring onions, lime rind and juice, cumin, Tabasco sauce, mayonnaise and salt and black pepper into a food processor or a blender for a few minutes and process until smooth.

2 Add the chopped coriander or parsley and process for a few more seconds. Spoon into a serving bowl, cover with clear film and chill in the fridge for 30 minutes, to let the flavours develop fully.

3 For the crudités, trim and peel the carrots. Halve the celery sticks lengthways and trim into sticks, the same length as the carrots. Quarter, core and thickly slice the apple and pear, then dip into the lemon or lime juice. Arrange with the baby sweetcorn on a platter.

NUTRITION NOTES

Per portion:
Energy	110Kcals/460kJ
Protein	6.22g
Fat	2.29g
Saturated Fat	0.49g
Fibre	6.73g

COOK'S TIP
Serve the guacamole dip with warmed wholemeal pitta bread.

4 Sprinkle the paprika over the guacamole and garnish with twisted lime slices.

TZATZIKI

Tzatziki is a Greek cucumber salad dressed with yogurt, mint and garlic. It is typically served with grilled lamb and chicken, but is also good served with crudités.

INGREDIENTS

Serves 4
1 cucumber
5ml/1 tsp salt
45ml/3 tbsp finely chopped fresh mint, plus a few sprigs to garnish
1 garlic clove, crushed
5ml/1 tsp caster sugar
200ml/7fl oz reduced fat Greek-style yogurt
cucumber flower, to garnish (optional)

1 Peel the cucumber. Reserve a little of the cucumber to use as a garnish if you wish and cut the rest in half lengthways. Remove the seeds with a teaspoon and discard. Slice the cucumber thinly and combine with salt. Leave for approximately 15–20 minutes. Salt will soften the cucumber and draw out any bitter juices.

2 Combine the mint, garlic, sugar and yogurt in a bowl, reserving a few sprigs of mint as decoration.

3 Rinse the cucumber in a sieve under cold running water to flush away the salt. Drain well and combine with the yogurt. Decorate with cucumber flower and/or mint. Serve cold.

NUTRITION NOTES

Per portion:
Energy	41.5Kcals/174.5kJ
Fat	0.51g
Saturated Fat	0.25g
Cholesterol	2mg
Fibre	0.2g

CHILLI TOMATO SALSA

This universal dip is great served with absolutely anything and can be made up to 24 hours in advance.

INGREDIENTS

Serves 4

1 shallot, peeled and halved
2 garlic cloves, peeled
handful of fresh basil leaves
500g/1¼ lb ripe tomatoes
10ml/2 tsp olive oil
2 green chillies
salt and black pepper

1 Place the shallot and garlic in a food processor with the fresh basil. Whizz the shallot, garlic and basil until finely chopped.

2 Halve the tomatoes and add to the food processor. Pulse the machine until the mixture is well blended and coarsely chopped.

3 With the motor running, slowly pour in the olive oil. Add salt and pepper to taste.

4 Halve the chillies lengthways and remove the seeds. Finely slice the chillies widthways into tiny strips and stir into the tomato salsa. Serve at room temperature.

NUTRITION NOTES	
Per portion:	
Energy	28Kcals/79kJ
Fat	0.47g
Saturated Fat	0.13g
Cholesterol	0
Fibre	1.45g

COOK'S TIP
The salsa is best made in the summer when tomatoes are at their best. In winter, use a drained 400g/14oz can of plum tomatoes.

MELON WITH WILD STRAWBERRIES

This fragrant, colourful starter is the perfect way to begin a rich meal as both melons and strawberries are virtually fat-free. Here several varieties are combined with strongly flavoured wild or woodland strawberries. If wild strawberries are not available, use ordinary strawberries or raspberries instead.

INGREDIENTS

Serves 4

1 cantaloupe or Charentais melon
1 Galia melon
900g/2lb watermelon
175g/6oz wild strawberries
4 sprigs fresh mint, to garnish

NUTRITION NOTES

Per portion:

Energy	42.5Kcals/178.6kJ
Fat	0.32g
Saturated Fat	0
Cholesterol	0
Fibre	1.09g

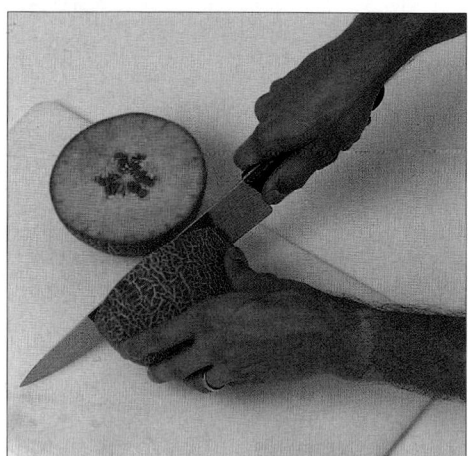

1 Using a large sharp knife, cut all three melons in half.

2 Scoop out the seeds from both the cantaloupe or Charentais and Galia melons with a spoon.

3 With a melon scoop, take out as many balls as you can from all three melons. Combine in a large bowl and chill for at least 1 hour.

4 Add the wild strawberries and mix together gently. Spoon out into four stemmed glass dishes.

5 Garnish each of the melon salads with a small sprig of mint and serve at once.

COOK'S TIP
Ripe melons should give slightly when pressed at the base, and should give off a sweet scent. Buy carefully if you plan to use the fruit on the day. If one or more varieties of melon aren't available, then substitute another, or buy two or three of the same variety – the salad might not be quite so colourful, but it will taste equally refreshing.

MUSSELS WITH THAI HERBS

Another simple dish to prepare. The lemon grass adds a refreshing tang to the mussels.

INGREDIENTS

Serves 6

1kg/2¼ lb mussels, cleaned and beards removed
2 lemon grass stalks, finely chopped
4 shallots, chopped
4 kaffir lime leaves, roughly torn
2 red chillies, sliced
15ml/1 tbsp fish sauce
30ml/2 tbsp lime juice
2 spring onions, chopped, and coriander leaves, to garnish

1 Put all the ingredients, except the spring onions and coriander, in a large saucepan and stir thoroughly.

2 Cover and cook for 5–7 minutes, shaking the saucepan occasionally, until the mussels open. Discard any mussels that do not open.

3 Transfer the cooked mussels to a serving platter.

4 Garnish the mussels with chopped spring onions and coriander leaves. Serve immediately.

NUTRITION NOTES	
Per portion:	
Energy	56Kcals/238kJ
Fat	1.22g
Saturated Fat	0.16g
Cholesterol	0.32g
Fibre	27g

PASTA WITH HERBY SCALLOPS

Low fat fromage frais, flavoured with mustard, garlic and herbs, makes a deceptively creamy sauce for pasta.

INGREDIENTS

Serves 4

120ml/4fl oz/½ cup low fat
  fromage frais
10ml/2 tsp wholegrain mustard
2 garlic cloves, crushed
30–45ml/2–3 tbsp fresh lime juice
60ml/4 tbsp chopped fresh parsley
30ml/2 tbsp snipped chives
350g/12oz black tagliatelle
12 large scallops
60ml/4 tbsp white wine
150ml/¼ pint/⅔ cup fish stock
salt and black pepper
lime wedges and parsley sprigs,
  to garnish

1 To make the sauce, mix the fromage frais, mustard, garlic, lime juice, parsley, chives and seasoning together in a mixing bowl.

2 Cook the pasta in a large pan of boiling salted water until *al dente*. Drain thoroughly.

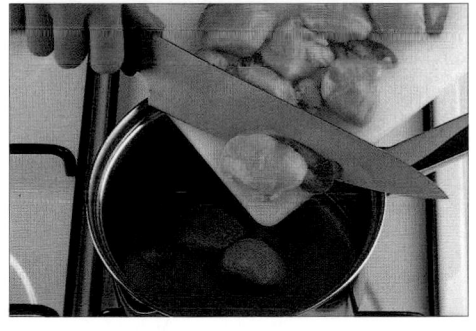

3 Slice the scallops in half, horizontally. Keep any coral whole. Put the wine and fish stock into a saucepan and heat to simmering point. Add the scallops and cook very gently for 3–4 minutes. (Don't cook for any longer, or they will toughen.)

COOK'S TIP
Black tagliatelle, made with squid ink, is available from Italian delicatessens, but other colours can be used to make this dish – try a mixture of white and green.

4 Remove the scallops. Boil the wine and stock to reduce by half and add the green sauce to the pan. Heat gently to warm, then return the scallops to the pan and cook for 1 minute. Spoon over the pasta and garnish with lime wedges and parsley.

NUTRITION NOTES

Per portion:

Energy	368Kcals/1561kJ
Fat	4.01g
Saturated Fat	0.98g
Cholesterol	99mg
Fibre	1.91g

FRESH FIG, APPLE AND DATE SALAD

Sweet Mediterranean figs and dates combine especially well with crisp eating apples. A hint of almond serves to unite the flavours, but if you'd prefer to reduce the fat even more, omit the marzipan and add another 30ml/2 tbsp low fat natural yogurt or use low fat fromage frais instead.

INGREDIENTS

Serves 4

6 large eating apples
juice of ½ lemon
175g/6oz fresh dates
25g/1oz white marzipan
5ml/1 tsp orange flower water
60ml/4 tbsp low fat natural yogurt
4 green or purple figs
4 almonds, toasted

1 Core the apples. Slice thinly, then cut into fine matchsticks. Moisten with lemon juice to keep them white.

NUTRITION NOTES

Per portion:

Energy	255Kcals/876.5kJ
Fat	4.98g
Saturated Fat	1.05g
Cholesterol	2.25mg
Fibre	1.69g

2 Remove the stones from the dates and cut the flesh into fine strips, then combine with the apple slices.

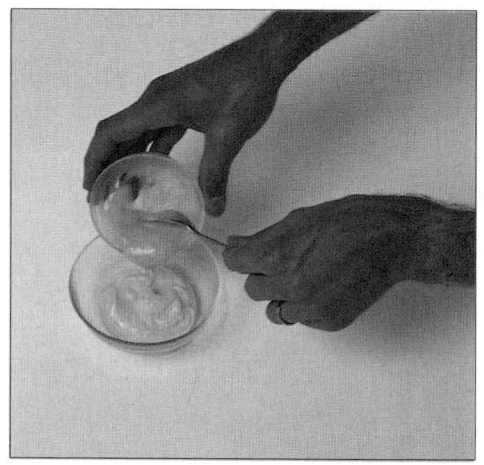

3 Soften the marzipan with orange flower water and combine with the yogurt. Mix well.

COOK'S TIP

For a slightly stronger almond flavour, add a few drops of almond essence to the yogurt mixture. When buying fresh figs, choose firm, unblemished fruit which give slightly when lightly squeezed. Avoid damaged, bruised or very soft fruit.

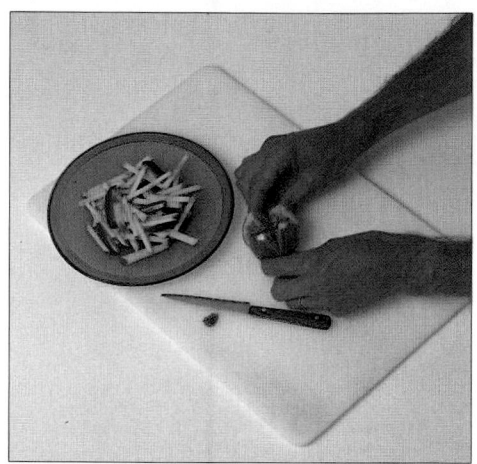

4 Pile the apples and dates in the centre of four plates. Remove the stem from each of the figs and divide the fruit into quarters without cutting right through the base. Squeeze the base with the thumb and forefinger of each hand to open up the fruit.

5 Place a fig in the centre of each salad. Spoon the yogurt filling on to the figs and decorate each one with a toasted almond.

CHEESE AND CHUTNEY TOASTIES

Quick cheese on toast can be made quite memorable with a few tasty additions. Serve these scrumptious toasties with a simple lettuce and cherry tomato salad.

— INGREDIENTS —

Serves 4
4 slices wholemeal bread, thickly sliced
85g/3½oz Cheddar cheese, grated
5ml/1 tsp dried thyme
30ml/2 tbsp chutney or relish
black pepper
salad, to serve

1 Toast the bread slices lightly on each side.

2 Mix the cheese and thyme together and season to taste with pepper.

NUTRITION NOTES	
Per portion:	
Energy	157.25Kcals/664.25kJ
Fat	4.24g
Saturated Fat	1.99g
Cholesterol	9.25mg
Fibre	2.41g

3 Spread the chutney or relish on the toast and divide the cheese evenly between the four slices.

4 Return the toast to the grill and cook until the cheese is browned and bubbling. Cut each slice into halves, diagonally, and serve at once with salad.

COOK'S TIP
If you prefer, use a reduced fat hard cheese, such as mature Cheddar or Red Leicester, in place of the full fat Cheddar to cut both calories and fat.

PARMA HAM AND PEPPER PIZZAS

The delicious flavours of these easy pizzas are hard to beat.

INGREDIENTS

Makes 4
½ loaf ciabatta bread
1 red pepper, roasted and peeled
1 yellow pepper, roasted and peeled
4 slices Parma ham, cut into
   thick strips
50g/2oz reduced fat mozzarella cheese
black pepper
tiny basil leaves, to garnish

NUTRITION NOTES

Per portion:
Energy	93Kcals/395kJ
Fat	3.25g
Saturated Fat	1.49g
Cholesterol	14mg
Fibre	1g

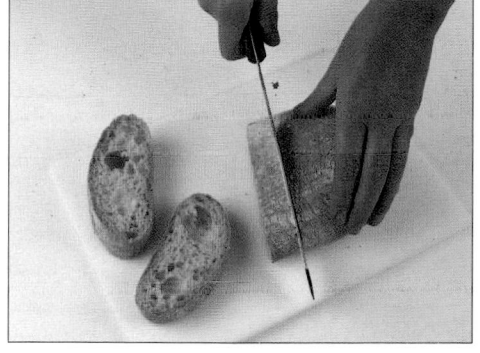

1 Cut the bread into four thick slices and toast until golden.

2 Cut the roasted peppers into thick strips and arrange on the toasted bread with the strips of Parma ham. Preheat the grill.

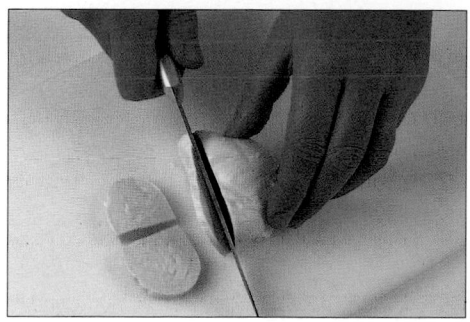

3 Thinly slice the mozzarella and arrange on top, then grind over plenty of black pepper. Grill for 2–3 minutes until the cheese is bubbling.

4 Scatter the basil leaves on top and serve immediately.

PASTA, PULSES AND GRAINS

Pasta, pulses and grains on their own are low in fat and a good source of carbohydrate, but they are often prepared with high fat ingredients and sauces. However, recipes do not need to be high in fat to be appetizing. There are delicious low fat recipes for pasta, such as Fusilli with Smoked Trout and Spaghetti with Chilli Bean Sauce. Pulses and grains, too, are a popular choice at mealtimes, and these recipes offer delicious and nutritious options, from Cracked Wheat and Mint Salad, to Spicy Bean Hot Pot.

TURKEY AND MACARONI CHEESE

A tasty low fat alternative to macaroni cheese, the addition of turkey rashers ensures this dish is a family favourite. Serve with warm ciabatta bread and a mixed leaf salad.

NUTRITION NOTES

Per portion:

Energy	152Kcals/637kJ
Fat	2.8g
Saturated Fat	0.7g
Cholesterol	12mg
Fibre	1.1g

INGREDIENTS

Serves 4

1 medium onion, chopped
150ml/¼ pint/⅔ cup vegetable or
 chicken stock
25g/1oz/2 tbsp low fat margarine
45ml/3 tbsp plain flour
300ml/½ pint/¼ cup skimmed milk
50g/2oz reduced fat Cheddar
 cheese, grated
5ml/1 tsp dry mustard
225g/8oz quick-cook macaroni
4 smoked turkey rashers, cut in half
2–3 firm tomatoes, sliced
a few fresh basil leaves
15ml/1 tbsp grated Parmesan cheese
salt and black pepper

1 Put the chopped onion and stock into a non-stick frying pan. Bring to the boil, stirring occasionally and cook for 5–6 minutes or until the stock has reduced entirely and the onion is transparent.

2 Put the margarine, flour, milk and seasoning into a saucepan and whisk together over the heat until thickened and smooth. Draw aside and add the cheese, mustard and onion.

3 Cook the macaroni in a large pan of boiling, salted water according to the instructions on the packet. Preheat the grill. Drain thoroughly and stir into the sauce. Transfer to a shallow oven-proof dish.

4 Arrange the turkey rashers and tomatoes overlapping on top of the macaroni cheese. Tuck in the basil leaves, then sprinkle with Parmesan and grill to lightly brown the top.

PASTA WITH TOMATO AND TUNA

INGREDIENTS

Serves 6

1 medium onion, finely chopped
1 celery stick, finely chopped
1 red pepper, seeded and diced
1 garlic clove, crushed
150ml/¼ pint/⅔ cup chicken stock
400g/14oz can chopped tomatoes
15ml/1 tbsp tomato purée
10ml/2 tsp caster sugar
15ml/1 tbsp chopped fresh basil
15ml/1 tbsp chopped fresh parsley
450g/1lb pasta shells
400g/14oz canned tuna in
   brine, drained
30ml/2 tbsp capers in vinegar, drained
salt and black pepper

1 Put the chopped onion, celery, red pepper and garlic into a pan. Add the stock, bring to the boil and cook for 5 minutes or until the stock has reduced almost completely.

2 Add the tomatoes, tomato purée, sugar and herbs. Season to taste and bring to the boil. Simmer for about 30 minutes until thick, stirring occasionally.

3 Meanwhile, cook the pasta in a large pan of boiling, salted water according to the packet instructions, until *al dente*. Drain thoroughly and transfer to a warm serving dish.

4 Flake the tuna fish into large chunks and add to the sauce with the capers. Heat gently for 1–2 minutes, pour over the pasta, toss gently and serve immediately.

COOK'S TIP
If fresh herbs are not available, use a 400g/14oz can of chopped tomatoes with herbs and add 5–10ml/1–2 tsp mixed dried herbs, in place of the fresh herbs.

NUTRITION NOTES
Per portion:

Energy	369Kcals/1549kJ
Fat	2.1g
Saturated Fat	0.4g
Cholesterol	34mg
Fibre	4g

CRAB PASTA SALAD

Low fat yogurt makes a piquant dressing for this salad.

INGREDIENTS

Serves 6
350g/12oz pasta twists
1 small red pepper, seeded and
    finely chopped
2 x 175g/6oz cans white crab
    meat, drained
115g/4oz cherry tomatoes, halved
¼ cucumber, halved, seeded and sliced
    into crescents
15ml/1 tbsp lemon juice
300ml/½ pint/1¼ cups low fat yogurt
2 celery sticks, finely chopped
10ml/2 tsp horseradish cream
2.5ml/½ tsp paprika
2.5ml/½ tsp Dijon mustard
30ml/2 tbsp sweet tomato pickle
    or chutney
salt and black pepper
fresh basil, to garnish

1 Cook the pasta in a large pan of boiling, salted water, according to the instructions on the packet, until *al dente*. Drain and rinse thoroughly under cold water.

2 Cover the chopped red pepper with boiling water and leave to stand for 1 minute. Drain and rinse under cold water. Pat dry on kitchen paper.

NUTRITION NOTES

Per portion:	
Energy	305Kcals/1283kJ
Fat	2.5g
Saturated Fat	0.5g
Cholesterol	43mg
Fibre	2.9g

3 Drain the crab meat and pick over carefully for pieces of shell. Put into a bowl with the halved tomatoes and sliced cucumber. Season with salt and pepper and sprinkle with lemon juice.

4 To make the dressing, add the red pepper to the yogurt, with the celery, horseradish cream, paprika, mustard and sweet tomato pickle or chutney. Mix the pasta with the dressing and transfer to a serving dish. Spoon the crab mixture on top and garnish with fresh basil.

Fusilli with Smoked Trout

Ingredients

Serves 4–6

2 carrots, cut in julienne sticks
1 leek, cut in julienne sticks
2 celery sticks, cut in julienne sticks
150ml/¼ pint/⅔ cup vegetable or
    fish stock
225g/8oz smoked trout fillets, skinned
    and cut into strips
200g/7oz low fat cream cheese
150ml/¼ pint/⅔ cup medium sweet
    white wine or fish stock
15ml/1 tbsp chopped fresh dill
    or fennel
225g/8oz fusilli (long, corkscrew pasta)
salt and black pepper
dill sprigs, to garnish

1 Put the carrots, leek and celery into a pan with the vegetable or fish stock. Bring to the boil and cook quickly for 4–5 minutes until the vegetables are tender and most of the stock has evaporated. Remove from the heat and add the smoked trout.

Nutrition Notes

Per portion:

Energy	339Kcals/1422kJ
Fat	4.7g
Saturated Fat	0.8g
Cholesterol	57mg
Fibre	4.1g

2 To make the sauce, put the cream cheese and wine or fish stock into a saucepan, heat and whisk until smooth. Season with salt and pepper. Add the chopped dill or fennel.

3 Cook the pasta according to the packet instructions in a large pan of boiling, salted water until *al dente*. Drain thoroughly.

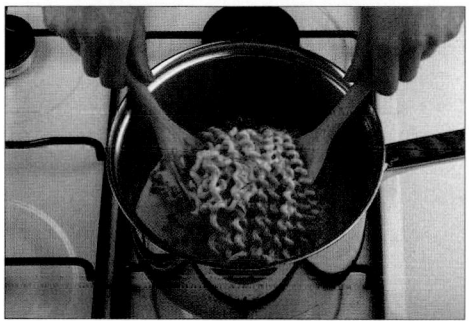

4 Return the pasta to the pan with the sauce, toss lightly and transfer to a serving bowl. Top with the cooked vegetables and trout. Serve at once garnished with dill sprigs.

Cook's Tip
When making the sauce, it is important to whisk it continuously while heating, to ensure a smooth result. Smoked salmon may be used in place of the trout, for a tasty change.

HOT SPICY PRAWNS WITH CAMPANELLE

This low fat prawn sauce tossed with hot pasta is an ideal supper-time dish. Add less or more chilli depending on how hot you like your food.

INGREDIENTS

Serves 4–6

225g/8oz tiger prawns, cooked
  and peeled
1–2 garlic cloves, crushed
finely grated rind of 1 lemon
15ml/1 tbsp lemon juice
1.5ml/¼ tsp red chilli paste or 1 large
  pinch of chilli powder
15ml/1 tbsp light soy sauce
150g/5oz smoked turkey rashers
1 shallot or small onion, finely chopped
60ml/4 tbsp dry white wine
225g/8oz campanelle or other
  pasta shapes
60ml/4 tbsp fish stock
4 firm ripe tomatoes, peeled, seeded
  and chopped
30ml/2 tbsp chopped fresh parsley
salt and black pepper

NUTRITION NOTES

Per portion:

Energy	331Kcals/1388kJ
Fat	2.9g
Saturated Fat	0.6g
Cholesterol	64mg
Fibre	3.2g

COOK'S TIP
To save time later, the prawns and marinade ingredients can be mixed together, covered and chilled in the fridge overnight, until ready to use.

1 In a glass bowl, mix the prawns with the garlic, lemon rind and juice, chilli paste or powder and soy sauce. Season with salt and pepper, cover and marinate for at least 1 hour.

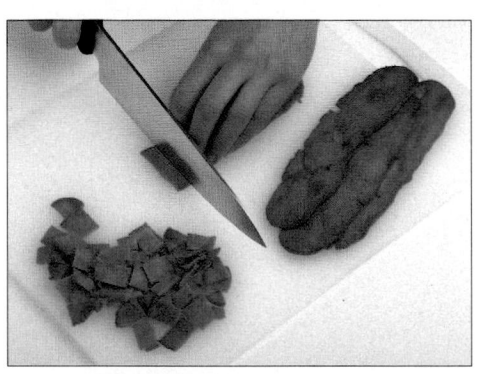

2 Grill the turkey rashers, then cut them into 5mm/¼in dice.

3 Put the shallot or onion and white wine into a pan, bring to the boil, cover and cook for 2–3 minutes or until they are tender and the wine has reduced by half.

4 Cook the pasta according to the packet instructions in a large pan of boiling, salted water until *al dente*. Drain thoroughly.

5 Just before serving, put the prawns with their marinade into a large frying pan, bring to the boil quickly and add the smoked turkey and fish stock. Heat through for 1 minute.

6 Add to the pasta with the chopped tomatoes and parsley, toss quickly and serve at once.

Tagliatelle with Mushrooms

Serves 4

1 small onion, finely chopped

2 garlic cloves, crushed

150ml/¼ pint/⅔ cup vegetable stock

225g/8oz mixed fresh mushrooms, such as field, chestnut, oyster or chanterelles

60ml/4 tbsp white or red wine

10ml/2 tsp tomato purée

15ml/1 tbsp soy sauce

5ml/1 tsp chopped fresh thyme

30ml/2 tbsp chopped fresh parsley, plus extra to garnish

225g/8oz fresh sun-dried tomato and herb tagliatelle

salt and black pepper

shavings of Parmesan cheese, to serve (optional)

1 Put the onion and garlic into a pan with the stock, then cover and cook for 5 minutes or until tender.

NUTRITION NOTES

Per portion:	
Energy	241Kcals/1010kJ
Fat	2.4g
Saturated Fat	0.7g
Carbohydrate	45g
Fibre	3g

2 Add the mushrooms (quartered or sliced if large or left whole if small), wine, tomato purée and soy sauce. Cover and cook for 5 minutes.

3 Remove the lid from the pan and boil until the liquid has reduced by half. Stir in the chopped fresh herbs and season to taste.

4 Cook the fresh pasta in a large pan of boiling, salted water for 2–5 minutes until *al dente*. Drain thoroughly and toss lightly with the mushrooms. Serve, garnished with parsley and shavings of Parmesan cheese, if you like.

PASTA PRIMAVERA

You can use any mixture of fresh, young spring vegetables to make this delicately flavoured pasta dish.

INGREDIENTS

Serves 4
225g/8oz thin asparagus spears,
 chopped in half
115g/4oz mange-tout, topped
 and tailed
115g/4oz baby sweetcorn
225g/8oz whole baby carrots, trimmed
1 small red pepper, seeded and chopped
8 spring onions, sliced
225g/8oz torchietti or other pasta shapes
150ml/¼ pint/⅔ cup low fat
 cottage cheese
150ml/¼ pint/⅔ cup low fat yogurt
15ml/1 tbsp lemon juice
15ml/1 tbsp chopped parsley
15ml/1 tbsp snipped chives
skimmed milk (optional)
salt and black pepper
sun-dried tomato bread, to serve

1 Cook the asparagus spears in a pan of boiling, salted water for 3–4 minutes. Add the mange-tout halfway through the cooking time. Drain and rinse both under cold water to stop further cooking.

2 Cook the baby corn, carrots, red pepper and spring onions in the same way until tender. Drain and rinse.

3 Cook the pasta in a large pan of boiling, salted water according to the packet instruction, until *al dente*. Drain thoroughly.

4 Put the cottage cheese, yogurt, lemon juice, parsley, chives and seasoning into a food processor or blender and process until smooth. Thin the sauce with skimmed milk, if necessary. Put into a large pan with the pasta and vegetables, heat gently and toss carefully. Serve at once with sun-dried tomato bread.

NUTRITION NOTES

Per portion:	
Energy	320Kcals/1344kJ
Fat	3.1g
Saturated Fat	0.4g
Cholesterol	3mg
Fibre	6.2g

Tagliatelle with Milanese Sauce

Ingredients

Serves 4

1 onion, finely chopped
1 celery stick, finely chopped
1 red pepper, seeded and diced
1–2 garlic cloves, crushed
150ml/¼ pint/⅔ cup vegetable or
  chicken stock
400g/14oz can tomatoes
15ml/1 tbsp tomato purée
10ml/2 tsp caster sugar
5ml/1 tsp mixed dried herbs
350g/12oz tagliatelle
115g/4oz button mushrooms, sliced
60ml/4 tbsp dry white wine
115g/4oz lean cooked ham, diced
salt and black pepper
15ml/1 tbsp chopped fresh parsley,
  to garnish

1 Put the chopped onion, celery, pepper and garlic into a saucepan. Add the stock, bring to the boil and cook for 5 minutes or until tender.

Cook's Tip

To reduce the calorie and fat content even more, omit the ham and use sweetcorn kernels or cooked broccoli florets instead.

2 Add the tomatoes, tomato purée, sugar and herbs. Season with salt and pepper. Bring to the boil and simmer for 30 minutes stirring occasionally, until the sauce is thick.

3 Cook the pasta in a large pan of boiling, salted water according to the packet instructions, until *al dente*. Drain thoroughly.

4 Put the mushrooms into a pan with the white wine, cover and cook for 3–4 minutes until the mushrooms are tender and all the wine has been absorbed.

5 Stir the mushrooms and ham into the tomato sauce and reheat gently over a low heat.

6 Transfer the pasta to a warmed serving dish and spoon on the sauce. Garnish with parsley.

Nutrition Notes

Per portion:

Energy	405Kcals/1700kJ
Fat	3.5g
Saturated Fat	0.8g
Cholesterol	17mg
Fibre	4.5g

SPAGHETTI WITH CHILLI BEAN SAUCE

A nutritious vegetarian option, ideal as a low fat main course.

INGREDIENTS

Serves 6

1 onion, finely chopped
1–2 garlic cloves, crushed
1 large green chilli, seeded
  and chopped
150ml/¼ pint/⅔ cup vegetable stock
400g/14oz can chopped tomatoes
30ml/2 tbsp tomato purée
120ml/4fl oz/½ cup red wine
5ml/1 tsp dried oregano
200g/7oz French beans, sliced
400g/14oz can red kidney
  beans, drained
400g/14oz can cannellini
  beans, drained
400g/14oz can chick-peas, drained
450g/1lb spaghetti
salt and black pepper

NUTRITION NOTES	
Per portion:	
Energy	431Kcals/1811kJ
Fat	3.6g
Saturated Fat	0.2g
Cholesterol	0
Fibre	9.9g

1 To make the sauce, put the chopped onion, garlic and chilli into a non-stick pan with the stock. Bring to the boil and cook for 5 minutes until tender.

2 Add the tomatoes, tomato purée, wine, seasoning and oregano. Bring to the boil, cover and simmer the sauce for 20 minutes.

3 Cook the French beans in boiling, salted water for about 5–6 minutes until tender. Drain thoroughly.

4 Add all the beans and the chick-peas to the sauce and simmer for a further 10 minutes. Meanwhile, cook the spaghetti in a large pan of boiling, salted water according to the individual packet instructions, until *al dente*. Drain thoroughly. Transfer the pasta to a serving dish or plates and top with the chilli bean sauce.

COOK'S TIP
Rinse canned beans thoroughly under cold, running water to remove as much salt as possible and drain well before use.

PINEAPPLE AND GINGER NOODLE SALAD

The tastes of the tropics are brought together in this appetizing noodle salad, ideal served as a lunch or suppertime dish.

INGREDIENTS

Serves 4

275g/10oz dried udon noodles
½ pineapple, peeled, cored and sliced
   into 4cm/1½in rings
45ml/3 tbsp soft light brown sugar
60ml/4 tbsp fresh lime juice
60ml/4 tbsp coconut milk
30ml/2 tbsp fish sauce
30ml/2 tbsp grated fresh root ginger
2 garlic cloves, finely chopped
1 ripe mango or 2 peaches, finely diced
black pepper
2 spring onions, finely sliced, 2 red
   chillies, seeded and finely shredded,
   plus mint leaves, to garnish

NUTRITION NOTES

Per portion:

Energy	350Kcals/1487kJ
Fat	4.49g
Saturated Fat	0.05g
Cholesterol	0
Fibre	3.13g

COOK'S TIP

Use 4–6 canned pineapple rings in fruit juice, if fresh pineapple is not available. If you haven't any fresh garlic, use 10ml/2 tsp ready-minced garlic instead. Choose ripe mangoes that have a smooth, unblemished skin and give slightly when you squeeze them gently.

1 Cook the noodles in a large saucepan of boiling water until tender, following the directions on the packet. Drain, then refresh under cold water and drain again.

3 Mix the lime juice, coconut milk and fish sauce in a salad bowl. Add the remaining brown sugar, with the ginger and garlic, and whisk well. Add the noodles and pineapple.

2 Place the pineapple rings in a flameproof dish, sprinkle with 30ml/2 tbsp of the sugar and grill for about 5 minutes, or until golden. Cool slightly and cut into small dice.

4 Add the mango or peaches to the bowl and toss well. Scatter over the spring onions, chillies and mint leaves before serving.

SPAGHETTI BOLOGNESE

INGREDIENTS

Serves 8

1 onion, chopped
2–3 garlic cloves, crushed
300ml/¹/₂ pint/1¹/₄ cups beef or
*   chicken stock*
450g/1lb extra-lean minced turkey
*   or beef*
2 x 400g/14oz cans chopped tomatoes
5ml/1 tsp dried basil
5ml/1 tsp dried oregano
60ml/4 tbsp tomato purée
450g/1lb button mushrooms, quartered
*   and sliced*
150ml/¹/₄ pint/²/₃ cup red wine
450g/1lb spaghetti
salt and black pepper

NUTRITION NOTES

Per portion:

Energy	321Kcals/1350kJ
Fat	4.1g
Saturated Fat	1.3g
Cholesterol	33mg
Fibre	2.7g

1 Put the chopped onion and garlic into a non-stick saucepan with half of the stock. Bring to the boil and cook for 5 minutes until the onion is tender and the stock has reduced completely.

COOK'S TIP
Sautéing vegetables in fat-free stock rather than oil is an easy way of saving calories and fat. Choose fat-free stock to reduce even more.

2 Add the turkey or beef and cook for 5 minutes, breaking up the meat with a fork. Add the tomatoes, herbs and tomato purée, bring to the boil, then cover and simmer for 1 hour.

3 Meanwhile, cook the mushrooms in a non-stick saucepan with the wine for 5 minutes or until the wine has evaporated. Add the mushrooms to the meat with salt and pepper to taste.

4 Cook the pasta in a large pan of boiling salted water for 8–12 minutes until tender. Drain thoroughly. Serve topped with the meat sauce.

RATATOUILLE PENNE BAKE

INGREDIENTS

Serves 6

1 small aubergine
2 courgettes, thickly sliced
200g/7oz firm tofu, cubed
45ml/3 tbsp dark soy sauce
1 garlic clove, crushed
10ml/2 tsp sesame seeds
1 small red pepper, seeded and sliced
1 onion, finely chopped
1–2 garlic cloves, crushed
150ml/¼ pint/⅔ cup vegetable stock
3 firm ripe tomatoes, skinned, seeded
   and quartered
15ml/1 tbsp chopped mixed herbs
225g/8oz penne or other pasta shapes
salt and black pepper
crusty bread, to serve

1 Wash the aubergine and cut into 2.5cm/1in cubes. Put into a colander with the courgettes, sprinkle with salt and leave to drain for 30 minutes.

2 Mix the tofu with the soy sauce, garlic and sesame seeds. Cover and marinate for 30 minutes.

3 Put the pepper, onion and garlic into a saucepan with the stock. Bring to the boil, cover and cook for 5 minutes until tender. Remove the lid and boil until all the stock has evaporated. Add the tomatoes and herbs to the pan and cook for a further 3 minutes, then add the rinsed aubergine and courgettes and cook until tender. Season to taste.

COOK'S TIP
Tofu is a low fat protein, but it is very bland. Marinating adds plenty of flavour – make sure you leave it for the full 30 minutes.

4 Meanwhile, cook the pasta in a large pan of boiling, salted water according to the packet instructions, until al dente, then drain thoroughly. Preheat the grill. Toss the pasta with the vegetables and tofu. Transfer to a shallow ovenproof dish and grill until lightly toasted. Serve with bread.

NUTRITION NOTES	
Per portion:	
Energy	208Kcals/873kJ
Fat	3.7g
Saturated Fat	0.5g
Cholesterol	0
Fibre	3.9g

SWEET AND SOUR PEPPERS WITH PASTA

A tasty and colourful low fat dish – perfect for lunch or supper.

INGREDIENTS

Serves 4

1 red, 1 yellow and 1 orange pepper
1 garlic clove, crushed
30ml/2 tbsp capers
30ml/2 tbsp raisins
5ml/1 tsp wholegrain mustard
rind and juice of 1 lime
5ml/1 tsp clear honey
30ml/2 tbsp chopped fresh coriander
225g/8oz pasta bows
salt and black pepper
shavings of Parmesan cheese, to serve
   (optional)

1 Quarter the peppers and remove the stalks and seeds. Put the quarters into boiling water and cook for 10–15 minutes, until tender. Drain and rinse under cold water, then peel off the skin and cut the flesh into strips lengthways.

2 Put the garlic, capers, raisins, mustard, lime rind and juice, honey, coriander and seasoning into a bowl and whisk together.

3 Cook the pasta in a large pan of boiling, salted water for 10–12 minutes, until *al dente*. Drain thoroughly.

4 Return the pasta to the pan and add the pepper strips and dressing. Heat gently, tossing to mix. Transfer to a warm serving bowl and serve with a few shavings of Parmesan cheese, if using.

NUTRITION NOTES

Per portion:

Energy	268Kcals/1125kJ
Fat	2.0g
Saturated Fat	0.5g
Cholesterol	1.3mg
Fibre	4.3g

PASTA WITH CHICK-PEA SAUCE

This is a delicious, and very speedy, low fat dish. The quality of canned pulses and tomatoes is so good that it is possible to transform them into a very fresh tasting pasta sauce in minutes. Choose whatever pasta shapes you like, although hollow shapes, such as penne (quills) or shells are particularly good with this sauce.

INGREDIENTS

Serves 6
450g/1lb penne or other pasta shapes
30ml/2 tsp olive oil
1 onion, thinly sliced
1 red pepper, seeded and sliced
400g/14oz can chopped tomatoes
425g/15oz can chick-peas
30ml/2 tbsp dry vermouth (optional)
5ml/1 tsp dried oregano
1 large bay leaf
30ml/2 tbsp capers
salt and black pepper
fresh oregano, to garnish

COOK'S TIP
Choose fresh or dried unfilled pasta for this dish. Whichever you choose, cook it in a large saucepan of water, so that the pasta keeps separate and doesn't stick together. Fresh pasta takes about 2–4 minutes to cook and dried pasta about 8–10 minutes. Cook pasta until it is *al dente* – firm and neither too hard nor too soft.

NUTRITION NOTES

Per portion:
Energy	268Kcals/1125kJ
Fat	2.0g
Saturated Fat	0.5g
Cholesterol	1.3mg
Fibre	4.3g

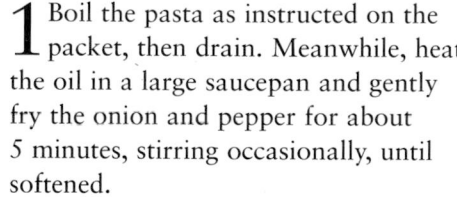

1 Boil the pasta as instructed on the packet, then drain. Meanwhile, heat the oil in a large saucepan and gently fry the onion and pepper for about 5 minutes, stirring occasionally, until softened.

2 Add the tomatoes, chick-peas with their liquid, vermouth (if liked), herbs and capers and stir well.

3 Season to taste and bring to the boil, then simmer for about 10 minutes. Remove the bay leaf and mix in the pasta. Reheat and serve hot, garnished with sprigs of oregano.

Pappardelle and Provençal Sauce

INGREDIENTS

Serves 4

2 small red onions
150ml/¼ pint/⅔ cup vegetable stock
1–2 garlic cloves, crushed
60ml/4 tbsp red wine
2 courgettes, cut in fingers
1 yellow pepper, seeded and sliced
400g/14oz can tomatoes
10ml/2 tsp fresh thyme
5ml/1 tsp caster sugar
350g/12oz pappardelle or other
   ribbon pasta
salt and black pepper
fresh thyme and 6 black olives, stoned
   and roughly chopped, to garnish

NUTRITION NOTES

Per portion:

Energy	369Kcals/1550kJ
Fat	2.5g
Saturated Fat	0.4g
Cholesterol	0
Fibre	4.3g

1 Cut each onion into eight wedges through the root end, to hold them together during cooking. Put into a saucepan with the stock and garlic. Bring to the boil, cover and simmer for 5 minutes until tender.

2 Add the red wine, courgettes, yellow pepper, tomatoes, thyme, sugar and seasoning. Bring to the boil and cook gently for 5–7 minutes, shaking the pan occasionally to coat the vegetables with the sauce. (Do not overcook the vegetables as they are much nicer if they remain slightly crunchy.)

3 Cook the pasta in a large pan of boiling, salted water according to the packet instructions, until *al dente*. Drain thoroughly.

4 Transfer the pasta to warmed serving plates and top with the vegetables. Garnish with fresh thyme and chopped black olives.

BASIC PASTA DOUGH
To make fresh pasta, sift 200g/ 7oz/1¾ cups plain flour and a pinch of salt on to a work surface and make a well in the centre. Break two eggs into the well, together with 10ml/2 tsp of cold water. Using a fork, beat the eggs gently, then gradually draw in the flour from the sides to make a thick paste. When the mixture becomes too stiff to use a fork, use your hands to mix to a firm dough. Knead for 5 minutes until smooth. Wrap in clear film and leave to rest for 20–30 minutes before rolling out and cutting.

SPAGHETTI ALLA CARBONARA

This is a variation on the classic charcoal burner's spaghetti, using turkey rashers and low fat cream cheese instead of the traditional bacon and egg.

INGREDIENTS

Serves 4

150g/5oz smoked turkey rashers
oil, for frying
1 medium onion, chopped
1–2 garlic cloves, crushed
150ml/¼ pint/⅔ cup chicken stock
150ml/¼ pint/⅔ cup dry white wine
200g/7oz low fat cream cheese
450g/1lb chilli and garlic-flavoured
　spaghetti
30ml/2 tbsp chopped fresh parsley
salt and black pepper
shavings of Parmesan cheese,
　to serve

1 Cut the turkey rashers into 1cm/½in strips. Fry quickly in a non-stick pan for 2–3 minutes. Add the onion, garlic and stock to the pan. Bring to the boil, cover and simmer for about 5 minutes until tender.

2 Add the wine and boil rapidly until reduced by half. Whisk in the cream cheese and season to taste.

4 Return the spaghetti to the pan with the sauce and parsley, toss well and serve immediately with a few thin shavings of Parmesan cheese.

COOK'S TIP
If you can't find chilli and garlic-flavoured spaghetti, use plain spaghetti and add a small amount of raw chilli and garlic in step 4 or use the pasta of your choice.

3 Meanwhile, cook the spaghetti in a large pan of boiling, salted water for 10–12 minutes until *al dente*. Drain thoroughly.

NUTRITION NOTES
Per portion:

Energy	500Kcals/2102kJ
Fat	3.3g
Saturated Fat	0.5g
Cholesterol	21mg
Fibre	4g

Fruity Ham and French Bread Pizza

French bread makes a great pizza base. For a really speedy recipe, use ready-prepared pizza topping instead of the tomato sauce and cook the pizzas under a hot grill for a few minutes to melt the cheese, instead of baking them in the oven.

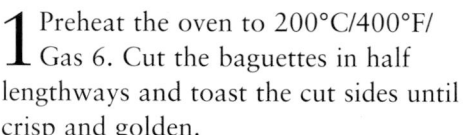

Ingredients

Serves 4
2 small baguettes
300ml/½ pint/1¼ cups tomato sauce
75g/3oz lean sliced cooked ham
4 canned pineapple rings, drained and chopped
½ small green pepper, seeded and cut into thin strips
50g/2oz reduced fat mature Cheddar cheese
salt and black pepper

1 Preheat the oven to 200°C/400°F/ Gas 6. Cut the baguettes in half lengthways and toast the cut sides until crisp and golden.

> **Cook's Tip**
> If you prefer, omit the ham and substitute cooked chicken, peeled prawns or tuna fish.

2 Spread the tomato sauce over the toasted baguettes.

3 Cut the ham into strips and lay on the baguettes with the pineapple and green pepper. Season to taste with salt and pepper.

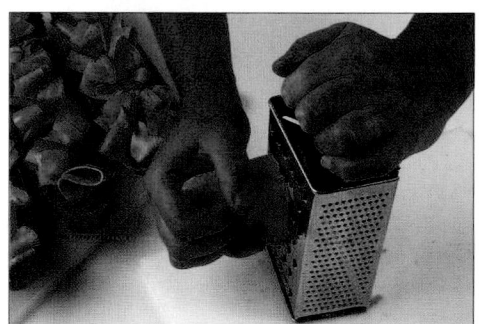

4 Grate the cheese and sprinkle on top. Bake for 15–20 minutes until crisp and golden.

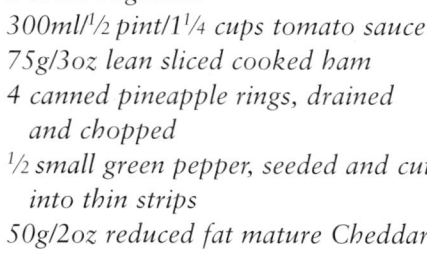

Nutrition Notes	
Per portion:	
Energy	111Kcals/468.7kJ
Fat	3.31g
Saturated Fat	1.63g
Cholesterol	18.25mg
Fibre	0.79g

CRACKED WHEAT AND MINT SALAD

Serves 4

250g/9oz/1⅔ cups cracked wheat
4 tomatoes
4 small courgettes, thinly sliced
    lengthways
4 spring onions, sliced on the diagonal
8 ready-to-eat dried apricots, chopped
40g/1½oz/¼ cup raisins
juice of 1 lemon
30ml/2 tbsp tomato juice
45ml/3 tbsp chopped fresh mint
1 garlic clove, crushed
salt and black pepper
sprig of fresh mint, to garnish

1 Put the cracked wheat into a large bowl. Add enough boiling water to come 2.5cm/1in above the level of the wheat. Leave to soak for 30 minutes, then drain well and squeeze out any excess water in a clean dish towel.

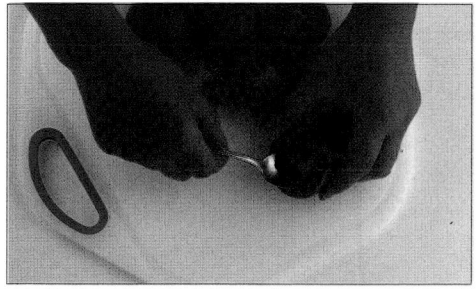

2 Meanwhile, plunge the tomatoes into boiling water for 1 minute and then into cold water. Slip off the skins. Halve, remove the seeds and cores and roughly chop the flesh.

3 Stir the chopped tomatoes, courgettes, spring onions, apricots and raisins into the cracked wheat.

4 Put the lemon and tomato juice, mint, garlic clove and seasoning into a small bowl and whisk together with a fork. Pour over the salad and mix well. Chill for at least 1 hour. Serve garnished with a sprig of mint.

NUTRITION NOTES	
Per portion:	
Energy	293Kcals/1231.7kJ
Fat	1.69g
Saturated Fat	0.28g
Fibre	2.25g

CHILLI BEAN BAKE

The contrasting textures of sauce, beans, vegetables and a crunchy cornbread topping make this a memorable meal.

INGREDIENTS

Serves 4

225g/8oz/1¼ cups red kidney beans
1 bay leaf
1 large onion, finely chopped
1 garlic clove, crushed
2 celery sticks, sliced
5ml/1 tsp ground cumin
5ml/1 tsp chilli powder
400g/14oz can chopped tomatoes
15ml/1 tbsp tomato purée
5ml/1 tsp dried mixed herbs
15ml/1 tbsp lemon juice
1 yellow pepper, seeded and diced
salt and black pepper
mixed salad, to serve

For the cornbread topping

175g/6oz/1½ cups corn meal
15ml/1 tbsp wholemeal flour
5ml/1 tsp baking powder
1 egg, beaten
175ml/6fl oz/¾ cup skimmed milk

1 Soak the beans overnight in cold water. Drain and rinse well. Pour 1 litre/1¾ pints/4 cups water into a large, heavy-based saucepan, add the beans and bay leaf and boil rapidly for 10 minutes. Lower the heat, cover and simmer for 35–40 minutes or until the beans are tender.

NUTRITION NOTES

Per portion:

Energy	399Kcals/1675kJ
Protein	22.86g
Fat	4.65g
Saturated Fat	0.86g
Fibre	11.59g

2 Add the onion, garlic, celery, cumin, chilli powder, chopped tomatoes, tomato purée and dried mixed herbs. Half cover the pan with a lid and simmer for a further 10 minutes.

3 Stir in the lemon juice, yellow pepper and seasoning. Simmer for a further 8–10 minutes, stirring occasionally, until the vegetables are just tender. Discard the bay leaf and spoon the mixture into a large casserole.

4 Preheat the oven to 220°C/425°F/ Gas 7. To make the topping, put the corn meal, flour, baking powder and a pinch of salt into a bowl and mix together. Make a well in the centre and add the egg and milk. Mix and pour over the bean mixture. Bake in the oven for 20 minutes or until brown. Serve hot with mixed salad.

SPICY BEAN HOT POT

INGREDIENTS

Serves 4

225g/8oz/3 cups button mushrooms
15ml/1 tbsp sunflower oil
2 onions, sliced
1 garlic clove, crushed
15ml/1 tbsp red wine vinegar
400g/14oz can chopped tomatoes
15ml/1 tbsp tomato purée
15ml/1 tbsp Worcestershire sauce
15ml/1 tbsp wholegrain mustard
15ml/1 tbsp soft dark brown sugar
250ml/8fl oz/1 cup vegetable stock
400g/14oz can red kidney
  beans, drained
400g/14oz can haricot or cannellini
  beans, drained
1 bay leaf
75g/3oz/¹/2 cup raisins
salt and black pepper
chopped fresh parsley, to garnish

1 Wipe the mushrooms, then cut them into small pieces. Set aside.

2 Heat the oil in a large saucepan or flameproof casserole, add the onions and garlic and cook over a gentle heat for 10 minutes until soft.

3 Add all the remaining ingredients except the mushrooms and seasoning. Bring to the boil, lower the heat and simmer for 10 minutes.

4 Add the mushrooms and simmer for 5 minutes more. Stir in salt and pepper to taste. Transfer to warm plates and sprinkle with parsley.

NUTRITION NOTES	
Per portion:	
Energy	280Kcals/1175kJ
Fat	4.5g
Saturated Fat	0.5g
Cholesterol	0

BEAN PURÉE WITH GRILLED CHICORY

The slightly bitter flavours of the radicchio and chicory make a wonderful marriage with the creamy bean purée. Walnut oil adds a nutty taste, but olive oil could also be used.

INGREDIENTS

Serves 4
400g/14oz can cannellini beans
45ml/3 tbsp low fat fromage frais
finely grated rind and juice of
    1 large orange
15ml/1 tbsp finely chopped
    fresh rosemary
4 heads of chicory
2 medium heads of radicchio
10ml/2 tbsp walnut oil
shreds of orange rind, to garnish
    (optional)

COOK'S TIP
Other suitable pulses to use are haricot, mung or broad beans.

1 Drain the beans, rinse, and drain again. Purée the beans in a blender or food processor with the fromage frais, orange rind, orange juice and rosemary. Set aside.

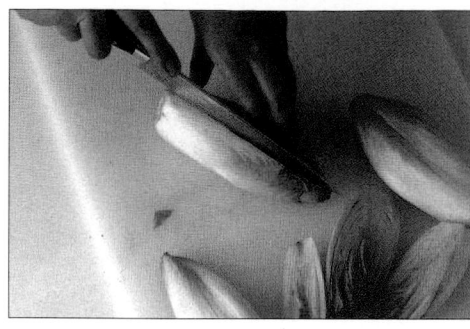

2 Cut the heads of chicory in half lengthwise.

3 Cut each radicchio head into eight wedges. Preheat the grill.

4 Lay out the chicory and radicchio on a baking tray and brush with the walnut oil. Grill for 2–3 minutes. Serve with the purée and scatter over the orange shreds, if using.

NUTRITION NOTES	
Per portion:	
Energy	103Kcals/432kJ
Protein	6.22g
Fat	1.54g
Saturated Fat	0.4g
Fibre	6.73g

LENTIL BOLOGNESE

A really useful sauce to serve with pasta, as a pancake stuffing or even as a protein-packed sauce for vegetables.

INGREDIENTS

Serves 6
45ml/3 tbsp olive oil
1 onion, chopped
2 garlic cloves, crushed
2 carrots, coarsely grated
2 celery sticks, chopped
115g/4oz/²⁄₃ cup red lentils
400g/14oz can chopped tomatoes
30ml/2 tbsp tomato purée
450ml/³⁄₄ pint/2 cups stock
15ml/1 tbsp fresh marjoram, chopped,
    or 5ml/1 tsp dried marjoram
salt and black pepper

1 Heat the oil in a large saucepan and gently fry the onion, garlic, carrots and celery for about 5 minutes, until they are soft.

NUTRITION NOTES

Per portion:

Energy	103Kcals/432kJ
Fat	2.19g
Saturated Fat	0.85g
Fibre	2.15g

2 Add the lentils, tomatoes, tomato purée, stock, marjoram and seasoning to the pan.

3 Bring the mixture to the boil, then partially cover with a lid and simmer for 20 minutes until thick and soft. Use the sauce as required.

COOK'S TIP
You can easily reduce the fat in this recipe by using less olive oil, or substituting a little of the stock and cooking the vegetables over a low heat in a non-stick frying pan until they are soft.

VEGETABLE BIRYANI

This exotic dish made from everyday ingredients will be appreciated by vegetarians and meat-eaters alike. It is extremely low in fat, but packed full of exciting flavours.

INGREDIENTS

Serves 4–6

175g/6oz/1 cup long grain rice
2 whole cloves
seeds of 2 cardamom pods
450ml/³⁄4 pint/scant 2 cups vegetable
   stock
2 garlic cloves
1 small onion, roughly chopped
5ml/1 tsp cumin seeds
5ml/1 tsp ground coriander
2.5ml/¹⁄2 tsp ground turmeric
2.5ml/¹⁄2 tsp chilli powder
1 large potato, peeled and cut into
   2.5cm/1in cubes
2 carrots, sliced
¹⁄2 cauliflower, broken into florets
50g/2oz French beans, cut into
   2.5cm/1in lengths
30ml/2 tbsp chopped fresh coriander
30ml/2 tbsp lime juice
salt and black pepper
sprig of fresh coriander, to garnish

NUTRITION NOTES

Per portion:

Energy	175Kcals/737kJ
Protein	3.66g
Fat	0.78g
Saturated Fat	0.12g
Fibre	0.58g

COOK'S TIP
Substitute other vegetables, if you like. Courgettes, broccoli, parsnip and sweet potatoes would all be excellent choices.

2 Reduce the heat, cover and simmer for 20 minutes, or until all the stock has been absorbed.

3 Meanwhile put the garlic cloves, onion, cumin seeds, coriander, turmeric, chilli powder and seasoning into a blender or coffee grinder together with 30ml/2 tbsp water. Blend to a smooth paste.

1 Put the rice, cloves and cardamom seeds into a large, heavy-based saucepan. Pour over the stock and bring to the boil.

4 Preheat the oven to 180°C/350°F/ Gas 4. Spoon the spicy paste into a flameproof casserole and cook over a low heat for 2 minutes, stirring occasionally.

5 Add the potato, carrots, cauliflower florets, beans and 90ml/6 tbsp water. Cover and cook over a low heat for a further 12 minutes, stirring occasionally. Add the chopped coriander.

6 Remove the cloves and spoon the rice over the vegetables. Sprinkle over the lime juice. Cover and cook in the oven for 25 minutes, or until the vegetables are tender. Fluff up the rice with a fork before serving and garnish with a sprig of fresh coriander.

COCONUT RICE

A delicious alternative to plain boiled rice, brown or white rice will both work well.

INGREDIENTS

Serves 6
450g/1lb/2 cups long grain rice
250ml/8fl oz/1 cup water
475ml/16fl oz/2 cups coconut milk
2.5ml/¹/₂ tsp salt
30ml/2 tbsp granulated sugar
fresh shredded coconut, to garnish

1 Wash the rice in cold water until it runs clear. Place the water, coconut milk, salt and sugar in a heavy-based saucepan or flameproof casserole.

COOK'S TIP
Coconut milk is available in cans, but if you cannot find it, use creamed coconut mixed with water according to the packet instructions.

2 Add the rice, cover and bring to the boil. Reduce the heat to low and simmer for about 15–20 minutes or until the rice is tender to the bite and cooked through.

3 Turn off the heat and allow the rice to rest in the saucepan for a further 5–10 minutes.

4 Fluff up the rice with chopsticks or a fork before serving garnished with shredded coconut.

NUTRITION NOTES	
Per portion:	
Energy	322.5Kcals/1371kJ
Fat	2.49g
Saturated Fat	1.45g
Cholesterol	0
Fibre	0.68g

JASMINE RICE

Perfectly cooked rice makes an ideal, low fat accompaniment to many low fat dishes such as vegetable chilli and vegetable bolognese.

INGREDIENTS

Serves 6

450g/1lb/2 cups long grain rice
750ml/1¼ pints/3 cups cold water
2.5ml/½ tsp salt

NUTRITION NOTES

Per portion:

Energy	270.8Kcals/1152kJ
Fat	0.75g
Saturated Fat	0
Cholesterol	0
Fibre	0.37g

COOK'S TIP
An electric rice cooker both cooks the rice and keeps it warm. Different sizes and models are available. The top of the range is a non-stick version, which is expensive, but well worth the money if you eat rice a lot.

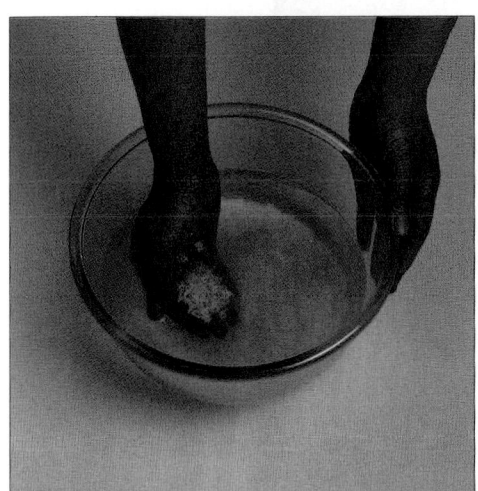

1 Rinse the rice in several changes of cold water until the water stays clear.

2 Put the rice in a heavy-based saucepan or flameproof casserole and add the water and salt. Bring the rice to a vigorous boil, uncovered, over a high heat.

3 Stir and reduce the heat to low. Cover and simmer for up to 20 minutes, or until all the water has been absorbed. Remove from the heat and leave to stand for 10 minutes.

4 Remove the lid and stir the rice gently with chopsticks or a fork to fluff up and separate the grains.

MEAT AND POULTRY

Make the most of the wide range of leaner cuts of meat available to make delicious, low fat dishes. Included here are tempting, light and nutritious main courses, which are packed with flavour, try spicy Thai Beef Salad or Tandoori Chicken Kebabs for an *al fresco* summer lunch, Ragoût of Veal, Chicken, Carrot and Leek Parcels or Venison with Cranberry Sauce for a special occasion dinner. If you are feeding a family, there are plenty of recipes here that will please, from Turkey and Tomato Hot Pot to Barbecued Chicken.

VENISON WITH CRANBERRY SAUCE

Venison steaks are now readily available. Lean and low in fat, they make a healthy choice for a special occasion. Served with a sauce of fresh seasonal cranberries, port and ginger, they make a dish with a wonderful combination of flavours.

INGREDIENTS

Serves 4

1 orange
1 lemon
75g/3oz/1 cup fresh or frozen
  cranberries
5ml/1 tsp grated fresh root ginger
1 thyme sprig, plus extra to garnish
5ml/1 tsp Dijon mustard
60ml/4 tbsp redcurrant jelly
150ml/¼ pint/⅔ cup ruby port
10ml/2 tsp sunflower oil
4 x 90g/3½oz venison steaks
2 shallots, finely chopped
salt and black pepper
mashed potato and broccoli, to serve

NUTRITION NOTES

Per portion:
Energy	250Kcals/1055.5kJ
Fat	4.39g
Saturated Fat	1.13g
Cholesterol	50mg
Fibre	1.59g

COOK'S TIP
When frying venison, always remember: the briefer the better. Venison will turn to leather if subjected to fierce heat after it has reached the medium-rare stage. If you dislike any hint of pink, cook it to this stage, then let it rest in a low oven for a few minutes.

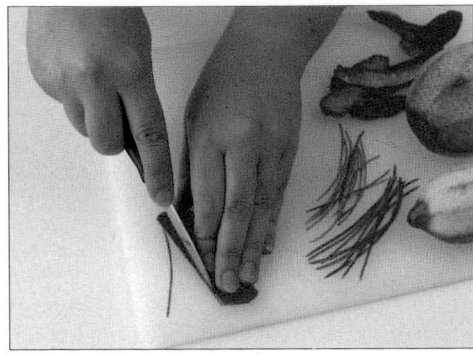

1 Pare the rind from half the orange and half the lemon using a vegetable peeler, then cut into very fine strips.

2 Blanch the strips in a small pan of boiling water for about 5 minutes until tender. Drain the strips and refresh under cold water.

3 Squeeze the juice from the orange and lemon, then pour into a small pan. Add the cranberries, ginger, thyme sprig, mustard, redcurrant jelly and port. Cook over a low heat until the jelly melts.

4 Bring the sauce to the boil, stirring occasionally, then cover the pan and reduce the heat. Cook gently for about 15 minutes, until the cranberries are just tender.

VARIATION
When fresh cranberries are unavailable, use redcurrants instead. Stir them into the sauce towards the end of cooking with the orange and lemon rinds.

5 Heat the oil in a heavy-based frying pan, add the venison steaks and cook over a high heat for 2–3 minutes.

6 Turn over the steaks and add the shallots to the pan. Cook the steaks on the other side for 2–3 minutes, depending on whether you like rare or medium-cooked meat.

7 Just before the end of cooking, pour in the sauce and add the strips of orange and lemon rind.

8 Leave the sauce to bubble for a few seconds to thicken slightly, then remove the thyme sprig and adjust the seasoning to taste.

9 Transfer the venison steaks to warmed plates and spoon over the sauce. Garnish with thyme sprigs and serve accompanied by mashed potato and broccoli.

DUCK BREAST SALAD

Tender slices of succulent cooked duck breasts served with a salad of mixed pasta, fruit and vegetables, tossed together in a light dressing, ensure that this gourmet dish will impress friends and family alike.

INGREDIENTS

Serves 6

2 small duck breasts, boned
5ml/1 tsp coriander seeds, crushed
350g/12oz rigatoni or penne pasta
150ml/¼ pint/⅔ cup fresh orange juice
15ml/1 tbsp lemon juice
10ml/2 tsp clear honey
1 shallot, finely chopped
1 garlic clove, crushed
1 celery stick, chopped
75g/3oz dried cherries
45ml/3 tbsp port
15ml/1 tbsp chopped fresh mint, plus extra to garnish
30ml/2 tbsp chopped fresh coriander, plus extra to garnish
1 eating apple, diced
2 oranges, segmented
salt and black pepper

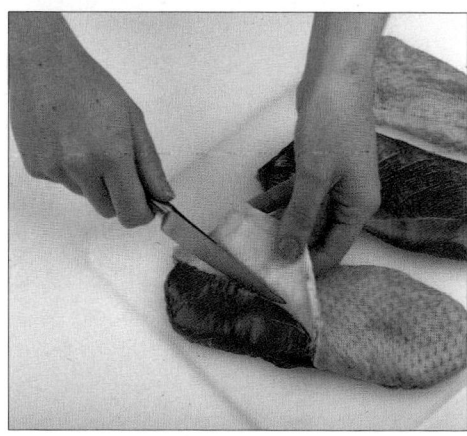

1 Remove the skin and fat from the duck breasts and season with salt and pepper. Rub with coriander seeds. Preheat the grill, then grill the duck for 10 minutes on each side. Wrap in foil and leave for 20 minutes.

COOK'S TIP
Choose skinless duck breasts to reduce fat and calories. Crush your own spices, such as coriander seeds, to create fresh, aromatic, spicy flavours. Ready-ground spices lose their flavour more quickly than whole spices, which are best freshly ground just before use.

2 Cook the pasta in a large pan of boiling, salted water according to the packet instructions, until *al dente*. Drain thoroughly and rinse under cold running water. Leave to cool.

3 To make the dressing, put the orange juice, lemon juice, honey, shallot, garlic, celery, cherries, port, mint and fresh coriander into a bowl, whisk together and leave to marinate for 30 minutes.

4 Slice the duck breasts very thinly. (They should be pink in the centre.)

5 Put the pasta into a large bowl, then add the dressing, diced apple and segments of orange. Toss well to coat the pasta. Transfer the salad to a serving plate with the duck slices and garnish with the extra mint and coriander.

NUTRITION NOTES	
Per portion:	
Energy	348Kcals/1460kJ
Fat	3.8g
Saturated Fat	0.9g
Cholesterol	55mg
Fibre	3g

TURKEY AND TOMATO HOT POT

Here, turkey is turned into tasty meatballs in a rich tomato sauce.

INGREDIENTS

Serves 4

25g/1oz white bread, crusts removed
30ml/2 tbsp skimmed milk
1 garlic clove, crushed
2.5ml/¹/₂ tsp caraway seeds
225g/8oz minced turkey
1 egg white
350ml/12fl oz/1¹/₂ cups chicken stock
400g/14oz can tomatoes
15ml/1 tbsp tomato purée
90g/3¹/₂oz/¹/₂ cup easy-cook rice
salt and black pepper
fresh basil, to garnish
carrot and courgette ribbons, to serve

1 Cut the bread into small cubes and put into a mixing bowl. Sprinkle over the milk and leave to soak for 5 minutes.

2 Add the garlic clove, caraway seeds, turkey and seasoning to the bread. Mix together well.

3 Whisk the egg white until stiff, then fold, half at a time, into the turkey mixture. Chill for 10 minutes.

4 While the turkey mixture is chilling, put the stock, tomatoes and tomato purée into a large saucepan and bring to the boil.

5 Add the rice, stir and cook briskly for about 5 minutes. Turn the heat down to a gentle simmer.

6 Meanwhile, shape the turkey mixture into 16 small balls. Carefully drop them into the tomato stock and simmer for a further 8–10 minutes, or until both the turkey balls and rice are cooked. Garnish with basil, and serve with carrot and courgette ribbons.

COOK'S TIPS

To make carrot and courgette ribbons, cut the vegetables lengthways into thin strips using a vegetable peeler, and blanch or steam until lightly cooked.

Lean minced turkey is low in fat and is a good source of protein. It makes an ideal base for this tasty low fat supper dish. Use minced chicken in place of turkey for an appetizing alternative.

NUTRITION NOTES

Per portion:

Energy	190Kcals/798kJ
Protein	18.04g
Fat	1.88g
Saturated Fat	0.24g
Fibre	10.4g

FISH AND SEAFOOD

The range of fresh fish available in our supermarkets is impressive, and fish is always a good choice for a healthy low fat diet. Most fish, particularly white fish, is low in fat and is a good source of protein. Oily fish contains more fat than white fish, but contains high levels of essential fatty acids which are vital for good health. Fish is quick and easy to prepare and cook and is ideal for serving with fresh seasonal vegetables as part of a healthy low fat meal. Try Cajun-style Cod, Herby Fishcakes with Lemon Sauce, Mediterranean Fish Cutlets or Curried Prawns in Coconut Milk – just some of the delicious, low fat recipes included in this chapter.

MONKFISH AND MUSSEL SKEWERS

Skinless white fish such as monkfish is a good source of protein whilst also being low in calories and fat. These attractive seafood kebabs, flavoured with a light marinade, are excellent grilled or barbecued and served with herby boiled rice and a mixed leaf salad.

INGREDIENTS

Serves 4
450g/1lb monkfish, skinned and boned
5ml/1 tsp olive oil
30ml/2 tbsp lemon juice
5ml/1 tsp paprika
1 garlic clove, crushed
4 turkey rashers
8 cooked mussels
8 raw prawns
15ml/1 tbsp chopped fresh dill
salt and black pepper
lemon wedges, to garnish
salad leaves and long grain and wild
    rice, to serve

1 Cut the monkfish into 2.5cm/1in cubes and place in a shallow glass dish. Mix together the oil, lemon juice, paprika and garlic clove and season.

2 Pour the marinade over the fish and toss to coat evenly. Cover and leave in a cool place for 30 minutes.

3 Cut the turkey rashers in half and wrap each strip around a mussel. Thread on to skewers, alternating with the fish cubes and raw prawns. Preheat the grill to high.

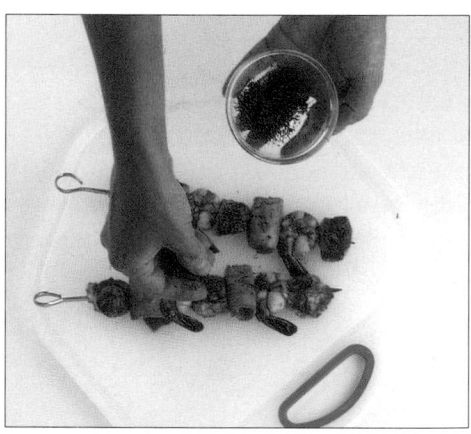

4 Grill the kebabs for 7–8 minutes, turning once and basting with the marinade. Sprinkle with chopped dill and salt. Garnish with lemon wedges and serve with salad and rice.

NUTRITION NOTES	
Per portion:	
Energy	133Kcals/560kJ
Protein	25.46g
Fat	3.23g
Saturated Fat	0.77g
Fibre	0.12g

LEMON SOLE BAKED IN A PAPER CASE

INGREDIENTS

Serves 4
*4 lemon sole fillets, each weighing
   about 150g/5oz*
½ small cucumber, sliced
4 lemon slices
60ml/4 tbsp dry white wine
sprigs of fresh dill, to garnish
potatoes and braised celery, to serve

For the yogurt hollandaise
150ml/¼ pint low fat natural yogurt
5ml/1 tsp lemon juice
2 egg yolks
5ml/1 tsp Dijon mustard
salt and black pepper

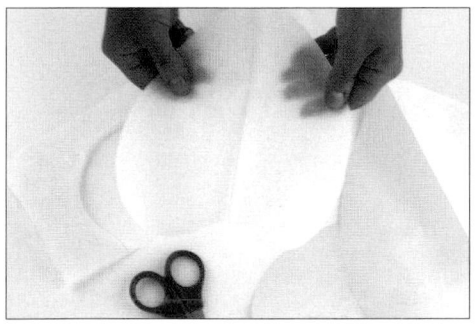

1 Preheat the oven to 180°C/350°F/
Gas 4. Cut out four heart shapes
from non-stick baking paper, each
about 20 x 15cm/8 x 6in.

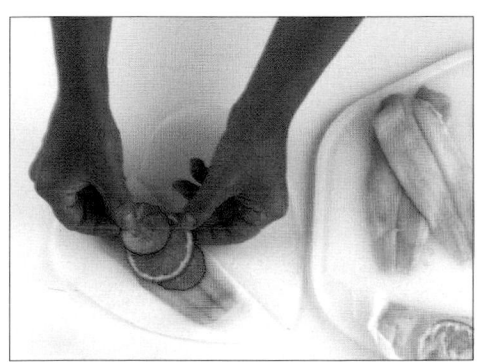

2 Place a sole fillet on one side of
each paper heart. Arrange the
cucumber and lemon slices on top of
each fillet. Sprinkle with the wine and
close the parcels by turning the edges of
the paper and twisting to secure. Put
on a baking tray and cook in the oven
for 15 minutes.

3 Meanwhile make the hollandaise.
Beat together the yogurt, lemon
juice and egg yolks in a double boiler
or bowl placed over a saucepan. Cook
over simmering water, stirring for
about 15 minutes, or until thickened.
(The sauce will become thinner after
10 minutes, but will thicken again.)

COOK'S TIP
Make sure that the paper parcels
are well sealed, so that none of
the delicious juices can escape.

4 Remove from the heat and stir in
the mustard. Season to taste with
salt and pepper. Open the fish parcels,
garnish with a sprig of dill and serve
accompanied with the sauce, new
potatoes and braised celery.

NUTRITION NOTES	
Per portion:	
Energy	185Kcals/779kJ
Protein	29.27g
Fat	4.99g
Saturated Fat	1.58g
Fibre	0.27g

HERBY FISHCAKES WITH LEMON SAUCE

The wonderful flavour of fresh herbs makes these fishcakes the catch of the day.

INGREDIENTS

Serves 4

350g/12oz potatoes, roughly chopped
75ml/5 tbsp skimmed milk
350g/12oz haddock or hoki
  fillets, skinned
15ml/1 tbsp lemon juice
15ml/1 tbsp creamed horseradish sauce
30ml/2 tbsp chopped fresh parsley
flour, for dusting
115g/4oz/2 cups fresh wholemeal
  breadcrumbs
salt and black pepper
flat leaf parsley sprigs, to garnish
sugar snap peas or mange-tout and a
  sliced tomato and onion salad,
  to serve

For the lemon and chive sauce
thinly pared rind and juice of
  ½ small lemon
120ml/4fl oz/½ cup dry white wine
2 thin slices of fresh root ginger
10ml/2 tsp cornflour
30ml/2 tbsp snipped fresh chives

NUTRITION NOTES

Per portion:
Energy	232Kcals/975kJ
Protein	19.99g
Fat	1.99g
Saturated Fat	0.26g
Fibre	3.11g

COOK'S TIP
Dry white wine is a tasty fat-free basis for this herby sauce. Try using cider as an alternative to wine, for a change.

1 Cook the potatoes in a large saucepan of boiling water for 15–20 minutes. Drain and mash with the milk and season to taste.

2 Purée the fish together with the lemon juice and horseradish sauce in a blender or food processor. Mix with the potatoes and parsley.

3 With floured hands, shape the mixture into eight fishcakes and coat with the breadcrumbs. Chill in the fridge for 30 minutes.

4 Preheat the grill to medium and cook the fishcakes for 5 minutes on each side, until browned.

5 To make the sauce, cut the lemon rind into julienne strips and put into a large saucepan together with the lemon juice, wine and ginger. Season to taste with salt and pepper.

6 Simmer, uncovered, for about 6 minutes. Blend the cornflour with 15ml/1 tbsp of cold water, add to the pan and simmer until clear. Stir in the chives immediately before serving.

7 Serve the sauce hot with the fishcakes, garnished with parsley sprigs and accompanied with mange-tout and a tomato and onion salad.

STEAMED FISH WITH CHILLI SAUCE

Steaming is one of the best – and lowest fat – methods of cooking fish. By leaving the fish whole and on the bone, you'll find that all the delicious flavour and moistness is retained.

INGREDIENTS

Serves 6
1 large or 2 medium, firm fish like bass
or grouper, scaled and cleaned
a fresh banana leaf or large piece
of foil
30ml/2 tbsp rice wine
3 red chillies, seeded and finely sliced
2 garlic cloves, finely chopped
2cm/³⁄₄in piece of fresh root ginger,
finely shredded
2 lemon grass stalks, crushed and
finely chopped
2 spring onions, chopped
30ml/2 tbsp fish sauce
juice of 1 lime

For the chilli sauce
10 red chillies, seeded and chopped
4 garlic cloves, chopped
60ml/4 tbsp fish sauce
15ml/1 tbsp sugar
75ml/5 tbsp lime juice

1 Rinse the fish under cold running water. Pat dry with kitchen paper. With a sharp knife, slash the skin of the fish a few times on both sides.

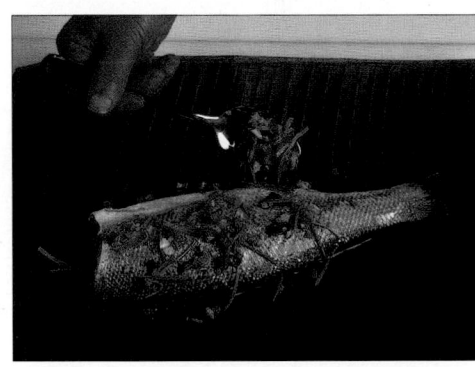

2 Place the fish on the banana leaf or foil. Mix together the remaining ingredients and spread over the fish.

3 Place a small upturned plate in the bottom of a wok or large frying pan, and add about 5cm/2in boiling water. Lay the banana leaf or foil with the fish on top on the plate and cover with a lid. Steam for about 10–15 minutes or until the fish is cooked.

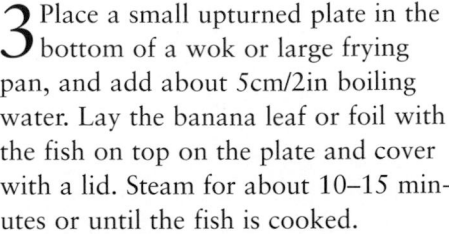

4 Meanwhile, put all the chilli sauce ingredients in a food processor and process until smooth. You may need to add a little cold water.

5 Serve the fish hot, on the banana leaf if liked, with the sweet chilli sauce to spoon over the top.

NUTRITION NOTES

Per portion:
Energy	170Kcals/721kJ
Fat	3.46g
Saturated Fat	0.54g
Cholesterol	106mg
Fibre	0.35g

BAKED COD WITH TOMATOES

For the very best flavour, use firm sun-ripened tomatoes for the sauce and make sure it is fairly thick before spooning it over the cod.

INGREDIENTS

Serves 4
10ml/2 tsp olive oil
1 onion, chopped
2 garlic cloves, finely chopped
450g/1lb tomatoes, peeled, seeded and chopped
5ml/1 tsp tomato purée
60ml/4 tbsp dry white wine
60ml/4 tbsp chopped flat leaf parsley
4 cod cutlets
30ml/2 tbsp dried breadcrumbs
salt and black pepper
new potatoes and green salad, to serve

NUTRITION NOTES

Per portion:
Energy	151Kcals/647kJ
Fat	1.5g
Saturated Fat	0.2g
Cholesterol	55.2mg
Fibre	2.42g

COOK'S TIP
For extra speed, use a 400g/14oz can of chopped tomatoes in place of the fresh tomatoes and 5–10ml/1–2 tsp ready-minced garlic in place of the garlic cloves.

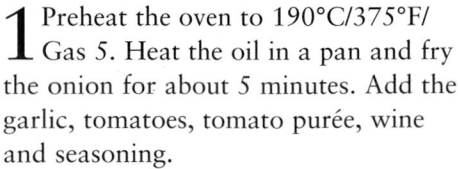

1 Preheat the oven to 190°C/375°F/ Gas 5. Heat the oil in a pan and fry the onion for about 5 minutes. Add the garlic, tomatoes, tomato purée, wine and seasoning.

2 Bring the sauce just to the boil, then reduce the heat slightly and cook, uncovered, for 15–20 minutes until thick. Stir in the parsley.

3 Grease an ovenproof dish, put in the cod cutlets and spoon an equal quantity of the tomato sauce on to each. Sprinkle the dried breadcrumbs over the top.

4 Bake for 20–30 minutes, basting the fish occasionally with the sauce, until the fish is tender and cooked through, and the breadcrumbs are golden and crisp. Serve hot with new potatoes and a green salad.

Pineapple Curry with Seafood

The delicate sweet and sour flavour of this curry comes from the pineapple, and although it seems an odd combination, it is delicious.

Ingredients

Serves 4

600ml/1 pint/2½ cups coconut milk
30ml/2 tbsp red curry paste
30ml/2 tbsp fish sauce
15ml/1 tbsp sugar
225g/8oz king prawns, shelled and deveined
450g/1lb mussels, cleaned and beards removed
175g/6oz fresh pineapple, finely crushed or chopped
5 kaffir lime leaves, torn
2 red chillies, chopped, and coriander leaves, to garnish

1 In a large saucepan, bring half the coconut milk to the boil and heat, stirring, until it separates.

2 Add the red curry paste and cook until fragrant. Add the fish sauce and sugar and continue to cook for a few moments.

3 Stir in the rest of the coconut milk and bring back to the boil. Add the king prawns, mussels, pineapple and kaffir lime leaves.

4 Reheat until boiling and then simmer for 3–5 minutes, until the prawns are cooked and the mussels have opened. Remove any mussels that have not opened and discard. Serve garnished with chillies and coriander.

Nutrition Notes	
Per portion:	
Energy	187Kcals/793kJ
Fat	3.5g
Saturated Fat	0.53g
Cholesterol	175.5mg
Fibre	0.59g

Curried Prawns in Coconut Milk

A curry-like dish where the prawns are cooked in a spicy coconut gravy with sweet and sour flavours from the tomatoes.

Ingredients

Serves 4

600ml/1 pint/2½ cups coconut milk
30ml/2 tbsp Thai curry paste
15ml/1 tbsp fish sauce
2.5ml/½ tsp salt
5ml/1 tsp sugar
450g/1lb shelled king prawns, tails left intact and deveined
225g/8oz cherry tomatoes
1 chilli, seeded and chopped
juice of ½ lime, to serve
chilli and coriander, to garnish

1 Put half the coconut milk into a pan or wok and bring to the boil.

2 Add the curry paste to the coconut milk, stir until it disperses, then simmer for about 10 minutes.

3 Add the fish sauce, salt, sugar and remaining coconut milk. Simmer for another 5 minutes.

Nutrition Notes	
Per portion:	
Energy	184Kcals/778kJ
Fat	3.26g
Saturated Fat	0.58g
Cholesterol	315mg
Fibre	0.6g

4 Add the prawns, cherry tomatoes and chilli. Simmer gently for about 5 minutes until the prawns are pink and tender.

5 Serve sprinkled with lime juice and garnish with sliced chilli and chopped coriander leaves.

TUNA AND MIXED VEGETABLE PASTA

INGREDIENTS

Serves 4
10ml/2 tsp olive oil
115g/4oz/1½ cups button
  mushrooms, sliced
1 garlic clove, crushed
½ red pepper, seeded and chopped
15ml/1 tbsp tomato paste
300ml/½ pint/1¼ cups tomato juice
115g/4oz/1 cup frozen peas
15–30ml/1–2 tbsp drained pickled
  green peppercorns, crushed
350g/12oz whole wheat pasta shapes
200g/7oz can tuna chunks in water,
  drained
6 spring onions, diagonally sliced

1 Heat the oil in a pan and gently sauté the mushrooms, garlic and pepper until softened. Stir in the tomato paste, then add the tomato juice, peas and some or all of the crushed peppercorns, depending on how spicy you like the sauce. Bring to the boil, lower the heat and simmer.

2 Bring a large saucepan of lightly salted water to the boil and cook the pasta for about 12 minutes (or according to the instructions on the package), until just tender. When the pasta is almost ready, add the tuna to the sauce and heat through gently. Stir in the spring onions. Drain the pasta, turn it into a heated bowl and pour over the sauce. Toss to mix. Serve at once.

NUTRITION NOTES	
Per portion:	
Energy	354Kcals/1514kJ
Fat	4.5g
Saturated Fat	0.67g
Cholesterol	22.95mg
Fibre	10.35g

SWEET AND SOUR FISH

White fish is high in protein, vitamins and minerals, but low in fat. Serve this tasty, nutritious dish with brown rice and stir-fried cabbage or spinach for a delicious lunch.

INGREDIENTS

Serves 4
60ml/4 tbsp cider vinegar
45ml/3 tbsp light soy sauce
50g/2oz/¼ cup granulated sugar
15ml/1 tbsp tomato purée
25ml/1½ tbsp cornflour
250ml/8fl oz/1 cup water
1 green pepper, seeded and sliced
225g/8oz can pineapple pieces in
  fruit juice
225g/8oz tomatoes, peeled and
  chopped
225g/8oz/2 cups button mushrooms,
  sliced
675g/1½lb chunky haddock fillets,
  skinned
salt and black pepper

1 Preheat the oven to 180°C/350°F/ Gas 4. Mix together the vinegar, soy sauce, sugar and tomato purée in a saucepan. Put the cornflour in a jug, stir in the water, then add the mixture to the saucepan, stirring well. Bring to the boil, stirring constantly until thickened. Lower the heat and simmer the sauce for 5 minutes.

2 Add the green pepper, canned pineapple pieces (with juice) and tomatoes to the pan and stir well. Mix in the mushrooms and heat through. Season to taste with salt and pepper.

3 Place the fish in a single layer in a shallow ovenproof dish, spoon over the sauce and cover with foil. Bake for 15–20 minutes until the fish is tender. Serve immediately.

NUTRITION NOTES	
Per portion:	
Energy	255Kcals/1070kJ
Fat	2g
Saturated Fat	0.5g
Cholesterol	61mg

VEGETABLES AND VEGETARIAN DISHES

Vegetarian food provides a tasty and nutritious choice at mealtimes for everyone and is especially tempting when it is low in fat too. Choose from delicious vegetable dishes such as Mixed Mushroom Ragoût, Devilled Onions en Croûte and Courgettes in Citrus Sauce or tempting low fat vegetarian meals such as Autumn Glory, Ratatouille Pancakes, and Tofu and Green Bean Curry.

HERBY BAKED TOMATOES

INGREDIENTS

Serves 4–6
675g/1½ lb large red and yellow
* tomatoes*
10ml/2 tsp red wine vinegar
2.5ml/½ tsp wholegrain mustard
1 garlic clove, crushed
10ml/2 tsp chopped fresh parsley
10ml/2 tsp snipped fresh chives
25g/1oz/½ cup fresh fine white
* breadcrumbs, for topping*
salt and black pepper

NUTRITION NOTES

Per portion:
Energy	37Kcals/156kJ
Fat	0.49g
Saturated Fat	0.16g
Cholesterol	0
Fibre	1.36g

1 Preheat the oven to 200°C/400°F/
Gas 6. Thickly slice the tomatoes
and arrange half of them in a 900ml/
1½ pint/3¾ cup ovenproof dish.

COOK'S TIP
Use wholemeal breadcrumbs in
place of white, for added colour,
flavour and fibre. Use 5–10ml/
1–2 tsp mixed dried herbs, if fresh
herbs are not available.

2 Mix the vinegar, mustard, garlic
and seasoning together. Stir in
10ml/2 tsp cold water. Sprinkle the
tomatoes with half the parsley and
chives, then drizzle over half the
dressing.

3 Lay the remaining tomato slices on
top, overlapping them slightly.
Drizzle with the remaining dressing.

4 Sprinkle over the breadcrumbs.
Bake for 25 minutes or until the
topping is golden. Sprinkle with the
remaining parsley and chives. Serve
immediately, garnished with sprigs
of parsley.

POTATO GRATIN

The flavour of Parmesan is wonderfully strong, so a little goes a long way. Leave the cheese out altogether for an almost fat-free dish.

INGREDIENTS

Serves 4
1 garlic clove
5 large baking potatoes, peeled
45ml/3tbsp freshly grated Parmesan
  cheese
600ml/1 pint/2½ cups vegetable or
  chicken stock
pinch of grated nutmeg
salt and black pepper

1 Preheat the oven to 200°C/400°F/ Gas 6. Halve the garlic clove and rub over the base and sides of a large shallow gratin dish.

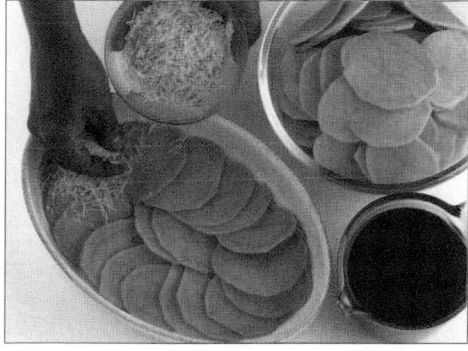

2 Slice the potatoes very thinly and arrange a third of them in the dish. Sprinkle with a little grated Parmesan cheese, and season with salt and pepper. Pour over some of the stock to prevent the potatoes from discolouring.

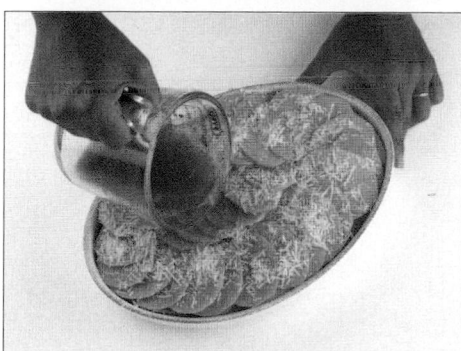

3 Continue layering the potatoes and cheese as before, then pour over the rest of the stock. Sprinkle with the grated nutmeg.

COOK'S TIP
For a potato and onion gratin, thinly slice one medium onion and layer with the potato.

4 Bake in the preheated oven for about 1¼–1½ hours or until the potatoes are tender and the tops well browned.

NUTRITION NOTES

Per portion:
Energy	178Kcals/749kJ
Protein	9.42g
Fat	1.57g
Saturated Fat	0.30g
Fibre	1.82g

MIXED MUSHROOM RAGOÛT

These mushrooms are delicious served hot or cold and can be prepared up to two days in advance.

INGREDIENTS

Serves 4

1 small onion, finely chopped
1 garlic clove, crushed
5ml/1 tsp coriander seeds, crushed
30ml/2 tbsp red wine vinegar
15ml/1 tbsp soy sauce
15ml/1 tbsp dry sherry
10ml/2 tsp tomato purée
10ml/2 tsp soft light brown sugar
150ml/1/4 pint/2/3 cup vegetable stock
115g/4oz baby button mushrooms
115g/4oz chestnut mushrooms,
  quartered
115g/4oz oyster mushrooms, sliced
salt and black pepper
coriander sprig, to garnish

NUTRITION NOTES

Per portion:
Energy	41Kcals/172kJ
Protein	2.51g
Fat	0.66g
Saturated Fat	0.08g
Fibre	1.02g

COOK'S TIP
There are many types of fresh mushrooms available and all are low in calories and fat. They add flavour and colour to many low fat dishes such as this tasty ragoût.

1 Put the first nine ingredients into a large saucepan. Bring to the boil and reduce the heat. Cover and simmer for 5 minutes.

2 Uncover the saucepan and simmer for 5 more minutes, or until the liquid has reduced by half.

3 Add the baby button and chestnut mushrooms and simmer for 3 minutes. Stir in the oyster mushrooms and cook for a further 2 minutes.

4 Remove the mushrooms from the pan with a slotted spoon and transfer them to a serving dish. Keep warm, if serving hot.

5 Boil the juices for about 5 minutes, or until reduced to about 75ml/5 tbsp. Season to taste.

6 Allow to cool for 2–3 minutes, then pour over the mushrooms. Serve hot or well chilled, garnished with a sprig of coriander.

DEVILLED ONIONS EN CROÛTE

Fill crisp bread cups with tender button onions tossed in a mustardy glaze. Try other low fat mixtures of vegetables, such as ratatouille, for a delicious change.

INGREDIENTS

Serves 4

12 thin slices of white or
 wholemeal bread
225g/8oz button onions or shallots
150ml/¼ pint/⅔ cup vegetable stock
15ml/1 tbsp dry white wine or
 dry sherry
2 turkey rashers, cut into thin strips
10ml/2 tsp Worcestershire sauce
5ml/1 tsp tomato purée
1.5ml/¼ tsp prepared English mustard
salt and black pepper
sprigs of flat leaf parsley, to garnish

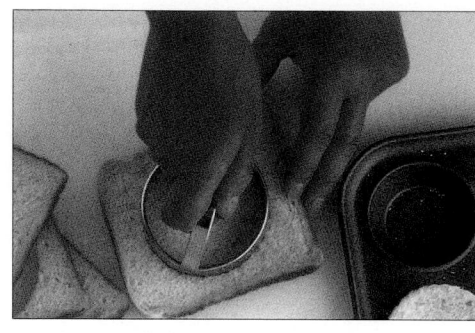

1 Preheat the oven to 200°C/400°F/ Gas 6. Stamp out the bread into rounds with a 7.5cm/3in fluted biscuit cutter and use to line a 12–cup patty tin.

2 Cover each bread case with non-stick baking paper and fill with baking beans. Bake blind for 5 minutes. Remove the paper and beans and bake for a further 5 minutes, until lightly browned and crisp.

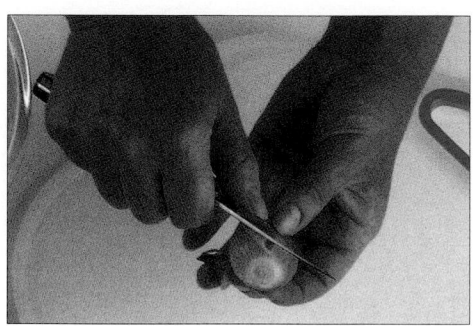

3 Meanwhile, put the button onions or shallots in a bowl and cover with boiling water. Leave for 3 minutes, then drain and rinse under cold water. Trim off their top and root ends and slip them out of their skins.

4 Simmer the onions and stock in a covered saucepan for 5 minutes. Uncover and cook, stirring occasionally until the stock has reduced entirely. Add all the remaining ingredients, except the flat leaf parsley, and cook for 2–3 minutes.

5 Fill the toast cups with the devilled onions. Serve hot, garnished with sprigs of flat leaf parsley.

NUTRITION NOTES	
Per portion:	
Energy	178Kcals/749kJ
Protein	9.42g
Fat	1.57g
Saturated Fat	0.30g
Fibre	1.82g

Kohlrabi Stuffed with Peppers

If you haven't sampled kohlrabi, or have only eaten it in stews where its flavour is lost, this dish is recommended. The slightly sharp flavour of the peppers are an excellent foil to the more earthy flavour of the kohlrabi.

Ingredients

Serves 4

4 small kohlrabies, about 175g–225g/
6–8oz each
about 400ml/14fl oz/²⁄₃ cup hot
vegetable stock
15ml/1 tbsp sunflower oil
1 onion, chopped
1 small red pepper, seeded and sliced
1 small green pepper, seeded and sliced
salt and black pepper
flat leaf parsley, to garnish (optional)

Nutrition Notes

Per portion:

Energy	112Kcals/470kJ
Fat	4.63g
Saturated Fat	0.55g
Cholesterol	0
Fibre	5.8g

1 Preheat the oven to 180°C/350°F/ Gas 4. Trim and top and tail the kohlrabies and arrange in the base of a medium-sized ovenproof dish.

2 Pour over the stock to come about halfway up the vegetables. Cover and braise in the oven for about 30 minutes, until tender. Transfer to a plate and allow to cool, reserving the stock.

3 Heat the oil in a frying pan and fry the onion for 3–4 minutes over a gentle heat, stirring occasionally. Add the peppers and cook for a further 2–3 minutes, until the onion is lightly browned.

4 Add the reserved vegetable stock and a little seasoning and simmer, uncovered, over a moderate heat until the stock has almost evaporated.

5 Scoop out the insides of the kohlrabies and chop roughly. Stir into the onion and pepper mixture, taste and adjust the seasoning. Arrange the shells in a shallow ovenproof dish.

6 Spoon the filling into the kohlrabi shells. Put in the oven for 5–10 minutes to heat through and then serve, garnished with a sprig of flat leaf parsley, if liked.

COURGETTES IN CITRUS SAUCE

If baby courgettes are unavailable, you can use larger ones, but they should be cooked whole so that they don't absorb too much water. After cooking, halve them lengthways and cut into 10cm/4in lengths. These tender, baby courgettes served in a very low fat sauce make this a tasty and low fat accompaniment to grilled fish fillets.

NUTRITION NOTES

Per portion:

Energy	33Kcals/138kJ
Protein	2.18g
Fat	0.42g
Saturated Fat	0.09g
Fibre	0.92g

INGREDIENTS

Serves 4

350g/12oz baby courgettes
4 spring onions, finely sliced
2.5cm/1in fresh root ginger, grated
30ml/2 tbsp cider vinegar
15ml/1 tbsp light soy sauce
5ml/1 tsp soft light brown sugar
45ml/3 tbsp vegetable stock
finely grated rind and juice of ½ lemon
    and ½ orange
5ml/1 tsp cornflour

1 Cook the courgettes in lightly salted boiling water for 3–4 minutes, or until just tender. Drain well.

2 Meanwhile, put all the remaining ingredients, except the cornflour, into a small saucepan and bring to the boil. Simmer for 3 minutes.

3 Blend the cornflour with 10ml/2 tsp cold water and add to the sauce. Bring to the boil, stirring continuously, until the sauce has thickened.

4 Pour the sauce over the courgettes and heat gently, shaking the pan to coat them evenly. Transfer to a warmed serving dish and serve.

COOK'S TIP
Use baby sweetcorn or aubergines in place of the courgettes for an appetizing change.

COURGETTE AND ASPARAGUS PARCELS

To appreciate the aroma, these paper parcels should be broken open at the table.

INGREDIENTS

Serves 4

2 medium courgettes
1 medium leek
225g/8oz young asparagus, trimmed
4 tarragon sprigs
4 whole garlic cloves, unpeeled
1 egg, beaten, to glaze
salt and black pepper

NUTRITION NOTES

Per portion:

Energy	110 Kcals/460kJ
Protein	6.22g
Fat	2.29g
Saturated Fat	0.49g
Fibre	6.73g

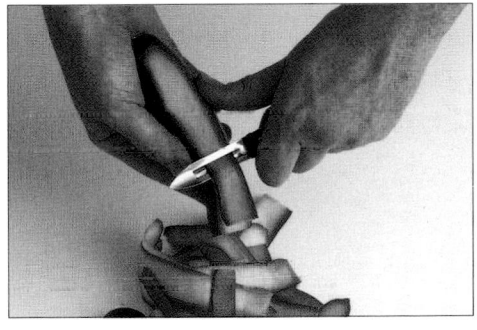

1 Preheat the oven to 200°C/400°F/ Gas 6. Using a potato peeler, carefully slice the courgettes lengthways into thin strips.

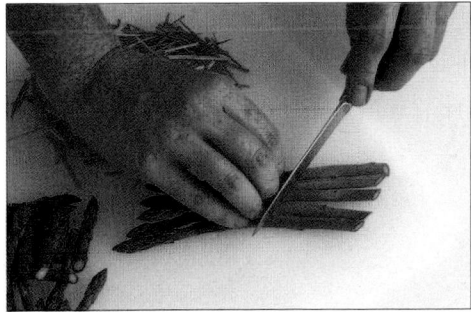

2 Cut the leek into very fine julienne strips and cut the asparagus evenly into 5cm/2in lengths.

3 Cut out four sheets of greaseproof paper measuring 30 x 38cm/ 12 x 15in and fold in half. Draw a large curve to make a heart shape when unfolded. Cut along the inside of the line and open out.

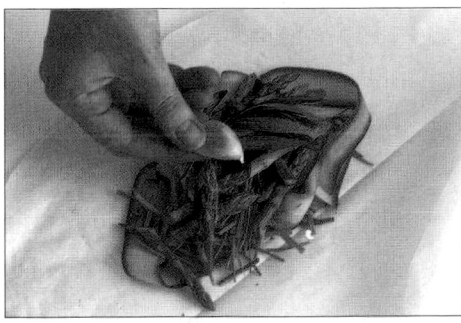

4 Divide the courgettes, asparagus and leek evenly between each paper heart, positioning the filling on one side of the fold line, and topping each with a sprig of tarragon and an unpeeled garlic clove. Season to taste.

5 Brush the edges lightly with the beaten egg and fold over.

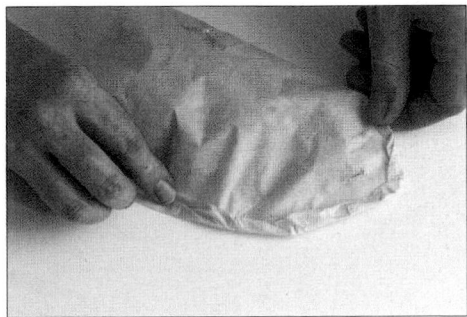

6 Twist the edges together so that each parcel is completely sealed. Lay the parcels on a baking sheet and cook for 10 minutes. Serve immediately.

COOK'S TIP
Experiment with other vegetable combinations, if you like.

AUTUMN GLORY

Glorious pumpkin shells summon up the delights of autumn and look too good to throw away, so use one as a serving pot. Pumpkin and pasta make marvellous partners, especially as a main course served from the baked shell.

INGREDIENTS

Serves 4–6

1 pumpkin, about 2kg/4–4¹/₂lb
1 onion, sliced
2.5cm/1in fresh root ginger
15ml/1 tbsp extra virgin olive oil
1 courgette, sliced
115g/4oz sliced mushrooms
400g/14oz can chopped tomatoes
75g/3oz/1 cup pasta shells
450ml/³/₄ pint/2 cups stock
60ml/4 tbsp fromage frais
30ml/2 tbsp chopped fresh basil
salt and black pepper

NUTRITION NOTES

Per portion (6 servings):	
Energy	140Kcals/588kJ
Fat	4.29g
Saturated Fat	1.17g
Cholesterol	2.5mg
Fibre	4.45g

COOK'S TIP

Use reduced fat or very low fat fromage frais to cut the calories and fat. Cook the onion, ginger and pumpkin flesh in 30–45ml/ 2–3 tbsp vegetable stock in place of the oil, to cut the calories and fat more.

1 Preheat the oven to 180°C/350°F/ Gas 4. Cut the top off the pumpkin with a large sharp knife, then scoop out and discard the seeds.

2 Using a small sharp knife and a sturdy tablespoon, extract as much of the pumpkin flesh as possible, then chop it into chunks.

3 Bake the pumpkin shell with its lid on for 45 minutes to 1 hour until the inside begins to soften.

4 Meanwhile make the filling. Gently fry the onion, ginger and pumpkin chunks in the olive oil for about 10 minutes, stirring occasionally.

5 Add the courgette and mushrooms and cook for a further 3 minutes, then stir in the tomatoes, pasta shells and stock. Season well, bring to the boil, then cover and simmer gently for another 10 minutes.

6 Stir the fromage frais and basil into the pasta and spoon the mixture into the pumpkin. (It may not be possible to fit all the filling into the pumpkin shell; serve the rest separately if this is the case.)

RATATOUILLE PANCAKES

These pancakes are made slightly thicker than usual to hold the juicy vegetable filling. By using cooking spray, you can control the amount of fat you are using and keep it to a minimum.

INGREDIENTS

Serves 4
75g/3oz/²⁄₃ cup plain flour
pinch of salt
25g/1oz/¹⁄₄ cup medium oatmeal
1 egg
300ml/¹⁄₂ pint/1¹⁄₄ cups skimmed milk
non-stick cooking spray
mixed salad, to serve

For the filling
1 large aubergine, cut into 2.5cm/
    1in cubes
1 garlic clove, crushed
2 medium courgettes, sliced
1 green pepper, seeded and sliced
1 red pepper, seeded and sliced
75ml/5 tbsp vegetable stock
200g/7oz can chopped tomatoes
5ml/1 tsp cornflour
salt and black pepper

NUTRITION NOTES

Per portion:
Energy	182Kcals/767kJ
Protein	9.36g
Fat	3.07g
Saturated Fat	0.62g
Fibre	4.73g

COOK'S TIP
Adding oatmeal to the batter mixture adds flavour, colour and texture to the cooked pancakes. If you like, wholemeal flour may be used in place of white flour to add extra fibre and flavour too.

1 Sift the flour and a pinch of salt into a bowl. Stir in the oatmeal. Make a well in the centre, add the egg and half the milk and mix to a smooth batter. Gradually beat in the remaining milk. Cover the bowl and leave to stand for 30 minutes.

2 Spray an 18cm/7in heavy-based frying pan with cooking spray. Heat the pan, then pour in just enough batter to cover the base of the pan thinly. Cook for 2–3 minutes, until the underside is golden brown. Flip over and cook for a further 1–2 minutes.

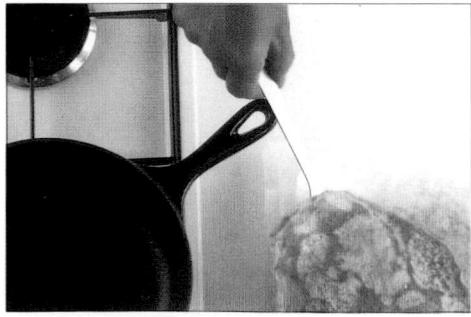

3 Slide the pancake out on to a plate lined with non-stick baking paper. Stack the other pancakes on top as they are made, interleaving each with non-stick baking paper. Keep warm.

4 For the filling, put the aubergine in a colander and sprinkle well with salt. Leave to stand on a plate for 30 minutes. Rinse thoroughly and drain well.

5 Put the garlic clove, courgettes, peppers, stock and tomatoes into a large saucepan. Simmer uncovered, stirring occasionally, for 10 minutes. Add the aubergine and cook for a further 15 minutes. Blend the cornflour with 10ml/2 tsp water and stir into the saucepan. Simmer for 2 minutes. Season to taste.

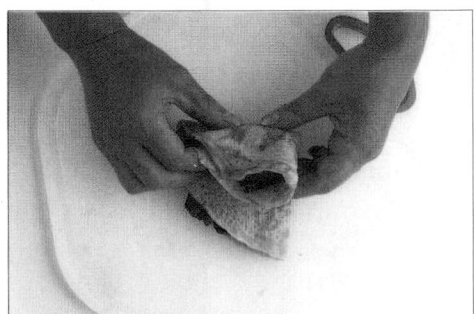

6 Spoon some of the ratatouille mixture into the middle of each pancake. Fold each one in half, then in half again to make a cone shape. Serve hot with a mixed salad.

Concertina Garlic Potatoes

With a low fat topping these would make a superb meal in themselves or could be enjoyed as a nutritious accompaniment to grilled fish or meat.

— Ingredients —

Serves 4

4 baking potatoes
2 garlic cloves, cut into slivers
60ml/4 tbsp low fat fromage frais
60ml/4 tbsp low fat natural yogurt
30ml/2 tbsp snipped chives
6–8 watercress sprigs, finely chopped
(optional)

— Nutrition Notes —

Per portion:
Energy	195Kcals/815kJ
Fat	3.5g
Saturated Fat	2g
Cholesterol	10mg

1 Preheat the oven to 200°C/400°F/ Gas 6. Slice each potato at about 5mm/¼in intervals, cutting not quite to the base, so that they retain their shape. Slip the slivers of the garlic between the cuts in the potatoes.

> Cook's Tip
> The most suitable potatoes for baking are of the floury variety. Some of the best include Estima, Cara and Kerr's Pink.

2 Place the garlic-filled potatoes in a roasting tin and bake for 1–1¼ hours or until soft when tested with a knife. Meanwhile, mix the low fat fromage frais and yogurt in a bowl, then stir in the snipped chives, along with the watercress, if using.

3 Serve the baked potatoes on individual plates, with a dollop of the yogurt and fromage frais mixture on top of each.

Potato, Leek and Tomato Bake

— Ingredients —

Serves 4

675g/1½lb potatoes
2 leeks, sliced
3 large tomatoes, sliced
a few fresh rosemary sprigs, crushed
1 garlic clove, crushed
300ml/½ pint/1¼ cups vegetable stock
15ml/1 tbsp olive oil
salt and black pepper

— Nutrition Notes —

Per portion:
Energy	180Kcals/740kJ
Fat	3.5g
Saturated Fat	0.5g
Cholesterol	0

1 Preheat the oven to 180°C/350°F/ Gas 4 and grease a 1.2 litre/ 2 pint/5 cup shallow ovenproof dish. Scrub and thinly slice the potatoes. Layer them with the leeks and tomatoes in the dish, scattering some rosemary between the layers and ending with a layer of potatoes.

2 Add the garlic to the stock, stir in salt if needed and pepper to taste, then pour over the vegetables. Brush the top layer of potatoes with olive oil.

3 Bake for 1¼–1½ hours until the potatoes are tender and the topping is golden and slightly crisp.

VEGETARIAN CASSOULET

Every town in south-west France has its own version of this popular classic. Warm French bread is all that you need to accompany this hearty low fat vegetable version.

INGREDIENTS

Serves 4–6

400g/14oz/2 cups dried haricot beans
1 bay leaf
2 onions
3 whole cloves
2 garlic cloves, crushed
5ml/1 tsp olive oil
2 leeks, thickly sliced
12 baby carrots
115g/4oz button mushrooms
400g/14oz can chopped tomatoes
15ml/1 tbsp tomato purée
5ml/1 tsp paprika
15ml/1 tbsp chopped fresh thyme
30ml/2 tbsp chopped fresh parsley
115g/4oz/2 cups fresh white
   breadcrumbs
salt and black pepper

NUTRITION NOTES

Per portion:

Energy	325Kcals/1378kJ
Fat	3.08g
Saturated Fat	0.46g
Cholesterol	0
Fibre	15.68g

COOK'S TIP

If you're short of time, use canned haricot beans – you'll need two 400g/14oz cans. Drain, reserving the bean juices and make up to 400ml/14fl oz/1²/₃ cups with vegetable stock.

1 Soak the beans overnight in plenty of cold water. Drain and rinse under cold running water. Put them in a saucepan with 1.75 litres/3 pints/7½ cups of cold water and the bay leaf. Bring to the boil and cook rapidly for 10 minutes.

2 Peel one of the onions and spike with the cloves. Add to the beans, then reduce the heat. Cover and simmer gently for 1 hour, until the beans are almost tender. Drain, reserving the stock but discarding the bay leaf and onion.

3 Chop the remaining onion and put it into a large flameproof casserole together with the crushed garlic and olive oil. Cook gently for 5 minutes, or until softened.

4 Preheat the oven to 160°C/325°F/Gas 3. Add the leeks, carrots, mushrooms, chopped tomatoes, tomato purée, paprika and thyme to the casserole, then pour in about 400ml/14fl oz/1²/₃ cups of the reserved stock.

5 Bring to the boil, cover and simmer gently for 10 minutes. Stir in the cooked beans and parsley. Season to taste with salt and pepper.

6 Sprinkle the breadcrumbs over the top and bake uncovered for 35 minutes or until the topping is golden brown and crisp.

SALADS

Salads are healthy and refreshing and can be served either as accompaniments to other dishes or as perfect low fat meals in themselves. Presented here is a wonderful selection of recipes: vegetarian delights include Marinated Cucumber Salad and a fresh, fast and filling Fruit and Fibre Salad; there are fish and seafood dishes, such as Prawn Noodle Salad and a tasty Thai-style Seafood Salad with Fragrant Herbs; and healthy salads made with grains and rice, such as Bulgur Wheat Salad with Oranges and Brown Rice Salad with Fruit, which are hearty enough to serve as a meal on their own.

MARINATED CUCUMBER SALAD

Sprinkling cucumbers with salt draws out some of the water and makes them softer and sweeter.

INGREDIENTS

Serves 6
2 medium cucumbers
15ml/1 tbsp salt
90g/3½oz/½ cup granulated sugar
175ml/6fl oz/¾ cup dry cider
15ml/1 tbsp cider vinegar
45ml/3 tbsp chopped fresh dill
pinch of pepper

NUTRITION NOTES

Per portion:	
Energy	111Kcals/465kJ
Fat	0.14g
Saturated Fat	0.01g
Fibre	0.62g

1 Slice the cucumbers thinly and place them in a colander, sprinkling salt between each layer. Put the colander over a bowl and leave to drain for 1 hour.

COOK'S TIP
As a shortcut, leave out the method for salting cucumber described in step 1.

2 Thoroughly rinse the cucumber under cold running water to remove excess salt, then pat dry on absorbent kitchen paper.

3 Gently heat the sugar, cider and vinegar in a saucepan, until the sugar has dissolved. Remove from the heat and leave to cool. Put the cucumber slices in a bowl, pour over the cider mixture and leave to marinate for about 2 hours.

4 Drain the cucumber and sprinkle with the dill and pepper to taste. Mix well and transfer to a serving dish. Chill in the fridge until ready to serve.

TURNIP SALAD WITH HORSERADISH

The robust-flavoured turnip partners well with the taste of horseradish and caraway seeds. This salad is delicious with cold roast beef or smoked trout.

INGREDIENTS

Serves 4

350g/12oz medium turnips
2 spring onions, white part only, chopped
15ml/1 tbsp caster sugar
salt
30ml/2 tbsp horseradish cream
10ml/2 tsp caraway seeds

NUTRITION NOTES

Per portion:	
Energy	48.25Kcals/204kJ
Fat	1.26g
Saturated Fat	0.09g
Cholesterol	1mg
Fibre	2.37g

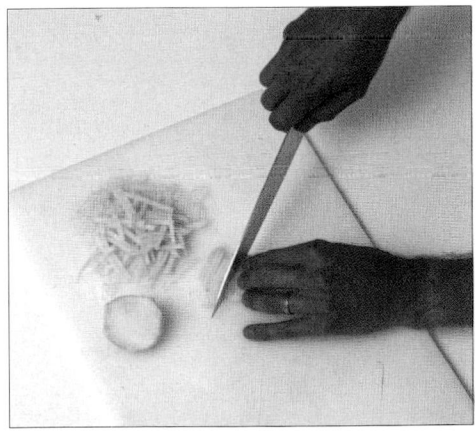

1 Peel, slice and shred the turnips – or grate them if you wish.

COOK'S TIP
If turnips are not available, giant white radish (mooli) can be used as a substitute. For extra sweetness, try red onion instead of spring onions.

2 Add the spring onions, sugar and salt, then rub together with your hands to soften the turnip.

3 Fold in the horseradish cream and caraway seeds and serve.

FRUIT AND FIBRE SALAD

Fresh, fast and filling, this salad makes a great supper or snack.

INGREDIENTS

Serves 6

225g/8oz red or white cabbage, or a
   mixture of both
3 medium carrots
1 pear
1 red-skinned eating apple
200g/7oz can green flageolet beans,
   drained
50g/2oz/¼ cup chopped dates

For the dressing

2.5ml/½ tsp dry English mustard
10ml/2 tsp clear honey
30ml/2 tbsp orange juice
5ml/1 tsp white wine vinegar
2.5ml/½ tsp paprika
salt and black pepper

1 Shred the cabbage very finely, discarding the core and tough ribs.

2 Cut the carrots into very thin strips, about 5cm/2in long.

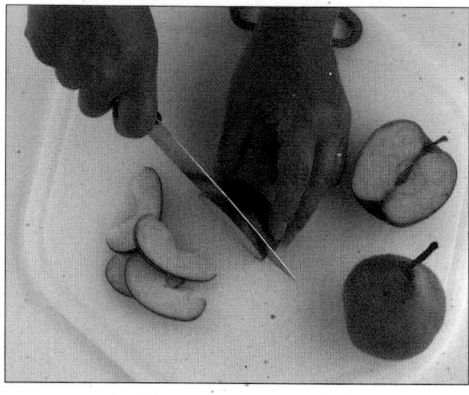

3 Quarter, core and slice the pear and the apple, leaving the peel on.

4 Put the fruit and vegetables in a bowl with the beans and dates. Mix well.

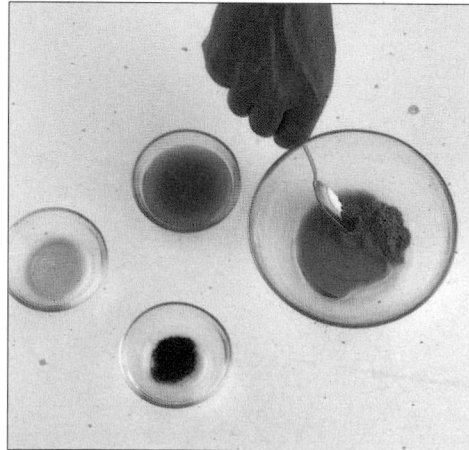

5 To make the dressing, blend the mustard with the honey until smooth. Add the orange juice, vinegar, paprika and seasoning and mix well.

6 Pour the dressing over the salad and toss to coat. Chill in the fridge for 30 minutes before serving.

NUTRITION NOTES

Per portion:

Energy	137Kcals/574kJ
Fat	0.87g
Saturated Fat	0.03g
Fibre	6.28g

COOK'S TIP
Use other canned beans, such as red kidney beans or chick-peas, in place of the flageolet beans. Add 2.5ml/½ tsp ground spice, such as chilli powder, cumin or coriander, for extra flavour. Add 5ml/1 tsp finely grated orange or lemon rind to the dressing, for extra flavour.

AUBERGINE SALAD

An appetizing and unusual salad that you will find yourself making over and over again.

INGREDIENTS

Serves 6
2 aubergines
15ml/1 tbsp oil
30ml/2 tbsp dried shrimps, soaked and drained
15ml/1 tbsp coarsely chopped garlic
30ml/2 tbsp freshly squeezed lime juice
5ml/1 tsp palm sugar
30ml/2 tbsp fish sauce
1 hard-boiled egg, chopped
4 shallots, thinly sliced into rings
coriander leaves, to garnish
2 red chillies, seeded and sliced, to garnish

COOK'S TIP
For an interesting variation, try using salted duck's or quail's eggs, cut in half, instead of chopped hen's eggs.

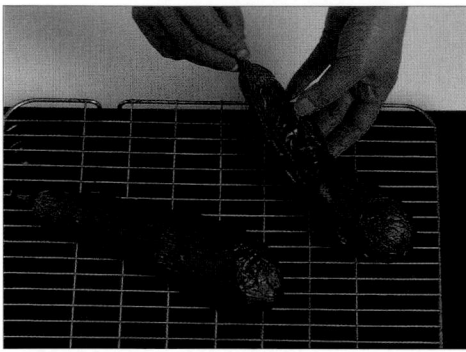

1 Grill or roast the aubergines until charred and tender.

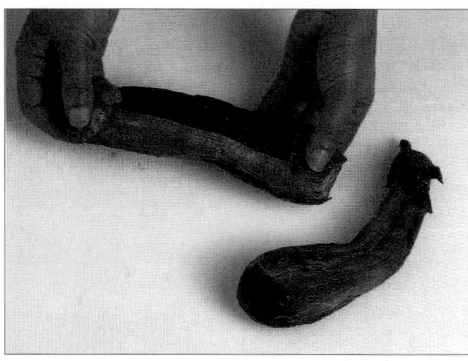

2 When cool enough to handle, peel away the skin and slice the aubergine into thick pieces.

3 Heat the oil in a small frying pan, add the drained shrimps and the garlic and fry until golden. Remove from the pan and set aside.

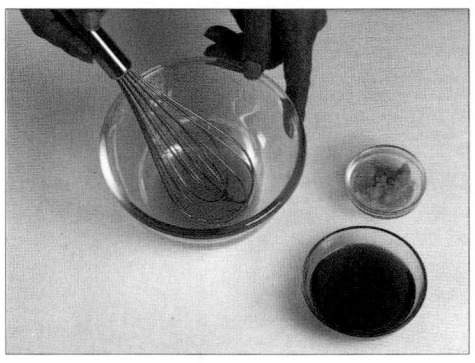

4 To make the dressing, put the lime juice, palm sugar and fish sauce in a small bowl and whisk together.

5 To serve, arrange the aubergine on a serving dish. Top with the chopped egg, shallot rings and dried shrimp mixture. Drizzle over the dressing and garnish with coriander and red chillies.

NUTRITION NOTES
Per portion:
Energy	70.5Kcals/295kJ
Fat	3.76g
Saturated Fat	0.68g
Cholesterol	57mg
Fibre	1.20g

BAMBOO SHOOT SALAD

This salad, which has a hot and sharp flavour, originated in north-east Thailand. Use fresh young bamboo shoots if you can find them, otherwise substitute canned bamboo shoots.

INGREDIENTS

Serves 4
400g/14oz can whole bamboo shoots
25g/1oz glutinous rice
30ml/2 tbsp chopped shallots
15ml/1 tbsp chopped garlic
45ml/3 tbsp chopped spring onions
30ml/2 tbsp fish sauce
30ml/2 tbsp lime juice
5ml/1 tsp granulated sugar
2.5ml/½ tsp dried flaked chillies
20–25 small mint leaves
15ml/1 tbsp toasted sesame seeds

1 Rinse and drain the bamboo shoots, then slice and set aside.

2 Dry roast the rice in a frying pan until it is golden brown. Remove and grind to fine crumbs with a pestle and mortar.

3 Tip the rice into a bowl, add the shallots, garlic, spring onions, fish sauce, lime juice, granulated sugar, chillies and half the mint leaves.

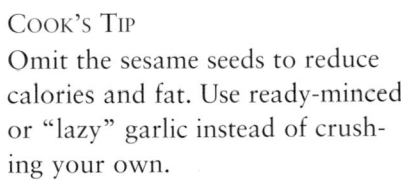

COOK'S TIP
Omit the sesame seeds to reduce calories and fat. Use ready-minced or "lazy" garlic instead of crushing your own.

4 Mix thoroughly, then pour over the bamboo shoots and toss together. Serve sprinkled with sesame seeds and the remaining mint leaves.

NUTRITION NOTES

Per portion:
Energy	73.5Kcals/308kJ
Fat	2.8g
Saturated Fat	0.41g
Cholesterol	0
Fibre	2.45g

BULGUR WHEAT SALAD WITH ORANGES

Bulgur wheat makes an excellent alternative to rice or pasta.

INGREDIENTS

Serves 6
1 small green pepper
150g/5oz/1 cup bulgur wheat
600ml/1 pint/2½ cups water
½ cucumber, diced
15g/½oz/½ cup chopped fresh mint
40g/1½oz/⅓ cup flaked almonds, toasted
grated rind and juice of 1 lemon
2 seedless oranges
salt and black pepper
mint sprigs, to garnish

1 Using a sharp vegetable knife, carefully halve and seed the green pepper. Cut it on a board into small cubes and put to one side.

2 Place the bulgur wheat in a saucepan and add the water. Bring to the boil, lower the heat, cover and simmer for 10–15 minutes until tender. Alternatively, place the bulgur wheat in a heatproof bowl, pour over boiling water and leave to soak for 30 minutes. Most, if not all, of the water should be absorbed; drain off any excess.

3 Toss the bulgur wheat with the cucumber, green pepper, mint and toasted almonds in a serving bowl. Add the grated lemon rind and juice.

4 Cut the rind from the oranges, then working over the bowl to catch the juice, cut the oranges into neat segments. Add to the bulgur mixture, then season and toss lightly. Garnish with the mint sprigs.

NUTRITION NOTES	
Per portion:	
Energy	160Kcals/672kJ
Fat	4.3g
Saturated Fat	0.33g
Cholesterol	0

BROWN RICE SALAD WITH FRUIT

An Oriental-style dressing gives this colourful rice salad extra piquancy. Whole grains like brown rice are unrefined, so they retain their natural fibre, vitamins and minerals.

— INGREDIENTS —

Serves 4–6

115g/4oz/²⁄₃ cup brown rice
1 small red pepper, seeded and diced
200g/7oz can sweetcorn niblets, drained
45ml/3 tbsp sultanas
225g/8oz can pineapple pieces in fruit juice
15ml/1 tbsp light soy sauce
5ml/1 tsp sunflower oil
10ml/2 tsp hazelnut oil
1 garlic clove, crushed
5ml/1 tsp finely chopped fresh root ginger
ground black pepper
4 spring onions, sliced, to garnish

> COOK'S TIP
> Hazelnut oil, which contains mainly monounsaturated fats, adds a wonderful flavour.

1 Cook the brown rice in a large saucepan of lightly salted boiling water for about 30 minutes, or until it is tender. Drain thoroughly and cool. Meanwhile, prepare the garnish by slicing the spring onions at an angle and setting aside.

2 Tip the rice into a bowl and add the red pepper, sweetcorn and sultanas. Drain the pineapple pieces, reserving the juice, add them to the rice mixture and toss lightly.

3 Pour the reserved pineapple juice into a clean screw-top jar. Add the soy sauce, sunflower and hazelnut oils, garlic and root ginger. Add some salt and pepper, then close the jar tightly and shake well to combine.

4 Pour the dressing over the salad and toss well. Scatter the spring onions over the top.

— NUTRITION NOTES —

Per portion:
Energy	245Kcals/1029kJ
Fat	4.25g
Saturated Fat	0.6g
Cholesterol	0

SEAFOOD SALAD WITH FRAGRANT HERBS

INGREDIENTS

Serves 6

250ml/8fl oz/1 cup fish stock or water
250g/12oz squid, cleaned and cut
   into rings
12 uncooked king prawns, shelled
12 scallops
50g/2oz bean thread noodles, soaked in
   warm water for 30 minutes
½ cucumber, cut into thin sticks
1 lemon grass stalk, finely chopped
2 kaffir lime leaves, finely shredded
2 shallots, finely sliced
juice of 1–2 limes
30ml/2 tbsp fish sauce
30ml/2 tbsp chopped spring onions
30ml/2 tbsp chopped coriander leaves
12–15 mint leaves, roughly torn
4 red chillies, seeded and sliced
coriander sprigs, to garnish

1 Pour the stock or water into a medium saucepan, set over a high heat and bring to the boil.

2 Cook each type of seafood separately in the stock. Don't overcook – it takes only a few minutes for each seafood. Remove and set aside.

3 Drain the bean thread noodles and cut them into short lengths, about 5cm/2in long. Combine the noodles with the cooked seafood.

4 Add all the remaining ingredients, mix together well and serve garnished with coriander sprigs.

NUTRITION NOTES

Per portion:
Energy	78Kcals/332kJ
Fat	1.12g
Saturated Fat	0.26g
Cholesterol	123mg
Fibre	0.37g

COOK'S TIP

Use other prepared seafood, such as mussels and cockles, in place of the prawns or scallops. If fresh chillies are not available, use 10–15ml/2–3 tsp of hot chilli powder or, alternatively, use ready-chopped chillies.

GREEN PAPAYA SALAD

There are many variations of this salad in south-east Asia. As green papaya is not easy to get hold of, shredded carrots, cucumber or green apple may be substituted. Serve this salad with raw white cabbage and rice.

INGREDIENTS

Serves 4
1 medium green papaya
4 garlic cloves
15ml/1 tbsp chopped shallots
3–4 red chillies, seeded and sliced
2.5ml/½ tsp salt
2–3 French or runner beans, cut into
  2cm/¾in lengths
2 tomatoes, cut into wedges
45ml/3 tbsp fish sauce
15ml/1 tbsp caster sugar
juice of 1 lime
30ml/2 tbsp crushed roasted peanuts
sliced red chillies, to garnish

1 Peel the papaya and cut in half lengthways, scrape out the seeds with a spoon and finely shred the flesh.

2 Grind the garlic, shallots, chillies and salt together in a large mortar with a pestle.

3 Add the shredded papaya a little at a time and pound until it becomes slightly limp and soft.

4 Add the sliced beans and tomatoes and lightly crush. Season with fish sauce, sugar and lime juice.

5 Transfer the salad to a serving dish, sprinkle with crushed peanuts and garnish with chillies.

NUTRITION NOTES

Per portion:
Energy	96Kcals/402kJ
Fat	4.2g
Saturated Fat	0.77g
Cholesterol	0

COOK'S TIP
If you do not have a large pestle and mortar, use a bowl and crush the shredded papaya with a wooden meat tenderizer or the end of a rolling pin.

THAI-STYLE CHICKEN SALAD

This salad comes from Chiang Mai, a city in the north-east of Thailand. It's hot and spicy, and wonderfully aromatic. Choose strong-flavoured leaves, such as curly endive or rocket, for the salad.

INGREDIENTS

Serves 6
450g/1lb minced chicken breast
1 lemon grass stalk, finely chopped
3 kaffir lime leaves, finely chopped
4 red chillies, seeded and chopped
60ml/4 tbsp lime juice
30ml/2 tbsp fish sauce
15ml/1 tbsp roasted ground rice
2 spring onions, chopped
30ml/2 tbsp coriander leaves
mixed salad leaves, cucumber and
   tomato slices, to serve
mint sprigs, to garnish

1 Heat a large non-stick frying pan. Add the minced chicken and cook in a little water.

2 Stir constantly until cooked, which will take about 7–10 minutes.

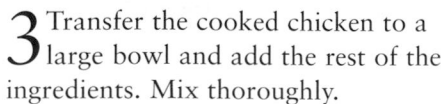

3 Transfer the cooked chicken to a large bowl and add the rest of the ingredients. Mix thoroughly.

4 Serve on a bed of mixed salad leaves, cucumber and tomato slices, garnished with mint sprigs.

COOK'S TIP
Use sticky (glutinous) rice to make roasted ground rice. Put the rice in a frying pan and dry roast until golden brown. Remove and grind to a powder with a pestle and mortar or in a food processor. Keep in a glass jar in a cool dry place and use as required.

NUTRITION NOTES

Per portion:
Energy	106Kcals/446kJ
Fat	1.13g
Saturated Fat	0.28g
Cholesterol	52.5mg
Fibre	0.7g

FRUITY PASTA AND PRAWN SALAD

Orange cantaloupe or
Charentais melon look
spectacular in this salad. Or
try a mixture of ogen,
cantaloupe and water melon.

INGREDIENTS

Serves 6

175g/6oz pasta shapes
225g/8oz/2 cups frozen prawns, thawed
*   and drained*
1 large or 2 small melons
30ml/2 tbsp olive oil
15ml/1 tbsp tarragon vinegar
30ml/2 tbsp snipped fresh chives or
*   chopped parsley*
herb sprigs, to garnish
shredded Chinese leaves, to serve

NUTRITION NOTES

Per portion:	
Energy	167Kcals/705kJ
Fat	4.72g
Saturated Fat	0.68g
Cholesterol	105mg
Fibre	2.08g

1 Cook the pasta in boiling salted
water according to the instructions
on the packet. Drain well and allow
to cool.

COOK'S TIP
Use wholewheat pasta in place
of white pasta, and mussels or
scallops in place of prawns.

2 Peel the prawns and discard the
shells.

3 Halve the melon(s) and remove the
seeds with a teaspoon. Scoop the
flesh into balls with a melon baller and
mix with the prawns and pasta.

4 Whisk the oil, vinegar and chopped
herbs together. Pour on to the
prawn mixture and turn to coat. Cover
and chill for at lesat 30 minutes.

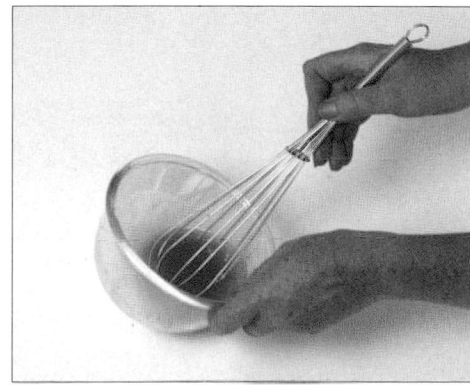

5 Meanwhile, shred the Chinese
leaves and use to line a shallow
bowl or the empty melon shells. Pile
the prawn mixture on to the Chinese
leaves and garnish with herb sprigs.

PRAWN NOODLE SALAD

A light, refreshing salad with all the tangy flavour of the sea. Instead of prawns, try squid, scallops, mussels or crab.

INGREDIENTS

Serves 4

115g/4oz cellophane noodles, soaked in hot water until soft
16 cooked prawns, peeled
1 small red pepper, seeded and cut into strips
½ cucumber, cut into strips
1 tomato, cut into strips
2 shallots, finely sliced
salt and black pepper
coriander leaves, to garnish

For the dressing

15ml/1 tbsp rice vinegar
30ml/2 tbsp fish sauce
30ml/2 tbsp fresh lime juice
pinch of salt
2.5ml/½ tsp grated fresh root ginger
1 lemon grass stalk, finely chopped
1 red chilli, seeded and finely sliced
30ml/2 tbsp roughly chopped mint
a few sprigs of tarragon, roughly chopped
15ml/1 tbsp snipped chives

1 Make the dressing by combining all the ingredients in a small bowl or jug; whisk well.

2 Drain the noodles, then plunge them in a saucepan of boiling water for 1 minute. Drain, rinse under cold running water and drain again well.

3 In a large bowl, combine the noodles with the prawns, red pepper, cucumber, tomato and shallots. Lightly season with salt and pepper, then toss with the dressing.

4 Spoon the noodles on to individual plates. Garnish with a few coriander leaves and serve at once.

NUTRITION NOTES

Per portion:

Energy	164.5Kcals/697kJ
Fat	2.9g
Saturated Fat	0.79g
Cholesterol	121mg
Fibre	1.86g

COOK'S TIP
Prawns are available ready-cooked and often shelled. To cook prawns, boil them for 5 minutes. Leave them to cool in the cooking liquid, then gently pull off the tail shell and twist off the head.

CACHUMBAR

Cachumbar is a salad relish most commonly served with Indian curries. There are many versions; this one will leave your mouth feeling cool and fresh after a spicy meal.

INGREDIENTS

Serves 4
3 ripe tomatoes
2 chopped spring onions
1.5ml/¼ tsp caster sugar
salt
45ml/3 tbsp chopped fresh coriander

NUTRITION NOTES

Per portion:	
Energy	9.5Kcals/73.5kJ
Fat	0.23g
Saturated Fat	0.07g
Cholesterol	0
Fibre	0.87g

1 Remove the tough cores from the bottom of the tomatoes with a small sharp-pointed knife.

COOK'S TIP
Cachumbar also makes a fine accompaniment to fresh crab, lobster and shellfish.

2 Halve the tomatoes, remove the seeds and dice the flesh.

3 Combine the tomatoes with the spring onions, sugar, salt and chopped coriander. Serve at room temperature.

HOT DESSERTS

When we talk of desserts and puddings we tend to imagine deliciously rich, creamy, calorie-laden treats which are well out of reach if you are following a low fat diet. However, it is very easy to create delicious, low fat desserts, full of flavour, colour and appeal that will satisfy a sweet tooth any day. We include a tasty selection of hot desserts, including temptations such as Sultana and Couscous Pudding, Baked Apples in Honey and Lemon, Cinnamon and Apricot Soufflés, Blueberry and Orange Crêpe Baskets, and Blushing Pears.

STRAWBERRY AND APPLE CRUMBLE

A high-fibre, healthier version of the classic apple crumble. Raspberries can be used instead of strawberries, either fresh or frozen.

INGREDIENTS

Serves 4
450g/1lb cooking apples
150g/5oz/1¼ cups strawberries
30ml/2 tbsp granulated sugar
2.5ml/½ tsp ground cinnamon
30ml/2 tbsp orange juice
custard or yogurt, to serve

For the crumble
45ml/3 tbsp plain wholemeal flour
50g/2oz/⅔ cup porridge oats
25g/1oz/⅛ cup low fat spread

1 Preheat the oven to 180°C/350°F/ Gas 4. Peel, core and slice the apples. Halve the strawberries.

NUTRITION NOTES

Per portion:
Energy	182.3Kcals/785kJ
Fat	4g
Saturated Fat	0.73g
Cholesterol	0.5mg
Fibre	3.87g

2 Toss together the apples, strawberries, sugar, cinnamon and orange juice. Tip into a 1.2 litre/ 2 pint/5 cup ovenproof dish, or four individual dishes.

3 Combine the flour and oats in a bowl and mix in the low fat spread with a fork.

4 Sprinkle the crumble evenly over the fruit. Bake for 40–45 minutes (20–25 minutes for individual dishes), until golden brown and bubbling. Serve warm with custard or yogurt.

SULTANA AND COUSCOUS PUDDING

Most couscous on the market now is the pre-cooked variety, which needs only the minimum of cooking, but check the packet instructions first to make sure. Serve hot, with yogurt or skimmed-milk custard.

INGREDIENTS

Serves 4
50g/2oz/⅓ cup sultanas
475ml/16fl oz/2 cups apple juice
90g/3½oz/1 cup couscous
2.5ml/½ tsp mixed spice

1 Lightly grease four 250ml/8fl oz/ 1 cup pudding basins or one 1 litre/1¾ pint/4 cup pudding basin. Put the sultanas and apple juice in a pan.

2 Bring the apple juice to the boil, then cover the pan and leave to simmer gently for 2–3 minutes to plump up the fruit. Using a slotted spoon, lift out about half the fruit and put it in the bottom of the basin(s).

3 Add the couscous and mixed spice to the pan and bring back to the boil, stirring. Cover and leave over a low heat for 8–10 minutes, or until the liquid has been absorbed.

NUTRITION NOTES	
Per portion:	
Energy	130.5Kcals/555kJ
Fat	0.40g
Saturated Fat	0
Cholesterol	0
Fibre	0.25g

4 Spoon the couscous into the basin(s), spread it level, then cover the basin(s) tightly with foil. Put the basin(s) in a steamer over boiling water, cover and steam for about 30 minutes. Run a knife around the edges, turn the puddings out carefully and serve.

COOK'S TIP
As an alternative, use chopped ready-to-eat dried apricots or pears, in place of the sultanas. Use unsweetened pineapple or orange juice in place of the apple juice.

CHUNKY APPLE BAKE

This filling, economical family pudding is a good way to use up slightly stale bread – any type of bread will do, but wholemeal is richer in fibre.

INGREDIENTS

Serves 4
450g/1lb cooking apples
75g/3oz wholemeal bread
115g/4oz/¹⁄₂ cup cottage cheese
45ml/3 tbsp light muscovado sugar
200ml/7fl oz/scant 1 cup semi-
  skimmed milk
5ml/1 tsp demerara sugar

NUTRITION NOTES

Per portion:
Energy	172.5Kcals/734.7kJ
Fat	2.5g
Saturated Fat	1.19g
Cholesterol	7.25mg
Fibre	2.69g

1 Preheat the oven to 220°C/425°F/ Gas 7. Peel the apples, cut them into quarters and remove the cores.

2 Roughly chop the apples into even-sized pieces, about 1cm/¹⁄₂in across.

3 Trim the crusts from the bread, then cut into 1cm/¹⁄₂in dice.

4 Toss together the apples, bread, cottage cheese and muscovado sugar.

5 Stir in the milk, then tip the mixture into a wide ovenproof dish. Sprinkle with the demerara sugar.

6 Bake the pudding for about 30–35 minutes, or until golden brown and bubbling. Serve hot.

COOK'S TIP
You may need to adjust the amount of milk used, depending on the dryness of the bread; the more stale the bread, the more milk it will absorb.

Baked Apples in Honey and Lemon

A classic mix of flavours in a healthy, traditional family pudding. Serve warm, with skimmed-milk custard or low fat frozen yogurt.

Nutrition Notes

Per portion:
Energy	61Kcals/259.5kJ
Fat	1.62g
Saturated Fat	0.42g
Cholesterol	0.25mg

Ingredients

Serves 4
4 medium cooking apples
15ml/1 tbsp clear honey
grated rind and juice of 1 lemon
15ml/1 tbsp low fat spread
skimmed-milk custard, to serve

1 Preheat the oven to 180°C/350°F/ Gas 4. Remove the cores from the apples, leaving them whole.

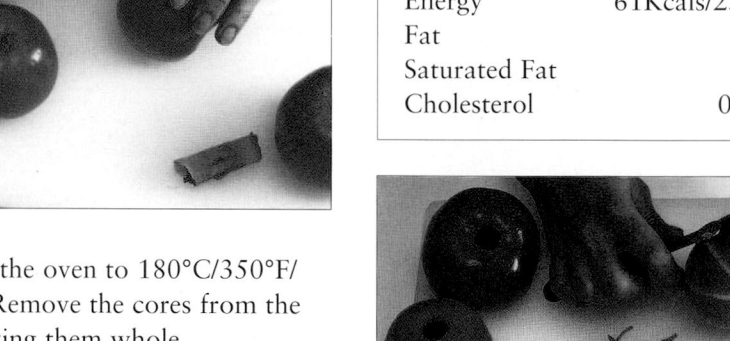

2 With a cannelle or sharp knife, cut lines through the apple skin at intervals. Put the apples in an oven-proof dish.

3 Mix together the honey, lemon rind, juice and low fat spread.

4 Spoon the mixture into the apples and cover the dish with foil or a lid. Bake for 40–45 minutes, or until the apples are tender. Serve with skimmed-milk custard.

APPLE AND BLACKCURRANT PANCAKES

These pancakes are made with a wholewheat batter and are filled with a delicious fruit mixture.

INGREDIENTS

Makes 10
115g/4oz/1 cup plain wholemeal flour
300ml/½ pint/1¼ cups skimmed milk
1 egg, beaten
15ml/1 tbsp sunflower oil, plus extra
for greasing
half fat crème fraîche, to serve
(optional)
toasted nuts or sesame seeds, for
sprinkling (optional)

For the filling
450g/1lb cooking apples
225g/8oz blackcurrants
30–45ml/2–3 tbsp water
30ml/2 tbsp demerara sugar

1 To make the pancake batter, put the flour in a mixing bowl and make a well in the centre.

2 Add a little of the milk with the egg and the oil. Beat the flour into the liquid, then gradually beat in the rest of the milk, keeping the batter smooth and free from lumps. Cover the batter and chill while you prepare the filling.

> **COOK'S TIP**
> If you wish, substitute other combinations of fruit for apples and blackcurrants.

3 Quarter, peel and core the apples. Slice them into a pan and add the blackcurrants and water. Cook over a gentle heat for 10–15 minutes until the fruit is soft. Stir in enough demerara sugar to sweeten.

NUTRITION NOTES	
Per portion:	
Energy	120Kcals/505kJ
Fat	3g
Saturated Fat	0.5g
Cholesterol	25mg

4 Lightly grease a non-stick pan with just a smear of oil. Heat the pan, pour in about 30ml/2 tbsp of the batter, swirl it around and cook for about 1 minute. Flip the pancake over with a palette knife and cook the other side. Put on a sheet of kitchen paper and keep hot while cooking the remaining pancakes.

5 Fill the pancakes with the apple and blackcurrant mixture and roll them up. Serve with a dollop of crème fraîche, if using, and sprinkle with nuts or sesame seeds, if liked.

CINNAMON AND APRICOT SOUFFLÉS

Don't expect these to be difficult simply because they're soufflés – they really couldn't be easier, and, best of all, they're very low in calories.

INGREDIENTS

Serves 4

3 eggs
115g/4oz/¹/₂ cup apricot fruit spread
finely grated rind of ¹/₂ lemon
5ml/1 tsp ground cinnamon
extra cinnamon, to decorate

NUTRITION NOTES

Per portion:

Energy	102Kcals/429kJ
Fat	4.97g
Saturated Fat	1.42g
Cholesterol	176.25mg
Fibre	0

1 Preheat the oven to 190°C/375°F/ Gas 5. Lightly grease four individual soufflé dishes and dust them lightly with flour.

2 Separate the eggs and put the yolks in a bowl with the fruit spread, lemon rind and cinnamon.

3 Whisk hard until the mixture is thick and pale in colour.

4 Place the egg whites in a clean bowl and whisk them until they are stiff enough to hold soft peaks.

5 Using a large metal spoon or spatula, fold the egg whites evenly into the yolk mixture.

6 Divide the soufflé mixture between the prepared dishes and bake for 10–15 minutes, until well risen and golden brown. Serve immediately, dusted with a little extra cinnamon.

COOK'S TIP
Puréed fresh or well-drained canned fruit can be used instead of the apricot spread, but make sure the mixture is not too wet, or the soufflés will not rise properly.

BLUEBERRY AND ORANGE CRÊPE BASKETS

Impress your guests with these pretty, fruit-filled crêpes. When blueberries are out of season, replace them with other soft fruit, such as raspberries.

INGREDIENTS

Serves 6
150g/5oz/1¼ cups plain flour
pinch of salt
2 egg whites
200ml/7fl oz/⅞ cup skimmed milk
150ml/¼ pint/⅔ cup orange juice
oil, for frying
yogurt or light crème fraîche, to serve

For the filling
4 medium oranges
225g/8oz/2 cups blueberries

1 Preheat the oven to 200°C/400°F/Gas 6. To make the pancakes, sift the flour and salt into a bowl. Make a well in the centre and add the egg whites, milk and orange juice. Whisk hard, until all the liquid has been incorporated and the batter is smooth and bubbly.

2 Lightly grease a heavy or non-stick pancake pan and heat it until it is very hot. Pour in just enough batter to cover the base of the pan, swirling it to cover the pan evenly.

3 Cook until the pancake has set and is golden, then turn it to cook the other side. Remove the pancake to a sheet of kitchen paper. Cook the remaining batter to make 6–8 pancakes.

4 Place six small ovenproof bowls or moulds on a baking sheet and lay the pancakes over these. Bake them in the oven for about 10 minutes, until they are crisp and set into shape. Lift the 'baskets' off the moulds.

5 Pare a thin piece of orange rind from one orange and cut it into fine strips. Blanch the strips in boiling water for 30 seconds, rinse them in cold water and set them aside. Cut all the peel and white pith from the oranges.

6 Divide the oranges into segments, catching the juice, combine with the blueberries and warm them gently. Spoon the fruit into the baskets and scatter the rind over the top. Serve with yogurt or light crème fraîche.

> **COOK'S TIP**
> Don't fill the pancake baskets until you're ready to serve them, because they will absorb the fruit juice and begin to soften.

NUTRITION NOTES

Per portion:
Energy	157.3Kcals/668.3kJ
Fat	2.20g
Saturated Fat	0.23g
Cholesterol	0.66mg
Fibre	2.87g

FILO CHIFFON PIE

Filo pastry is low in fat and is very easy to use. Keep a pack in the freezer, ready to make impressive desserts like this one.

INGREDIENTS

Serves 6
500g/1¼lb rhubarb
5ml/1 tsp mixed spice
finely grated rind and juice of 1 orange
15ml/1 tbsp granulated sugar
15g/½oz/1 tbsp butter
3 filo pastry sheets

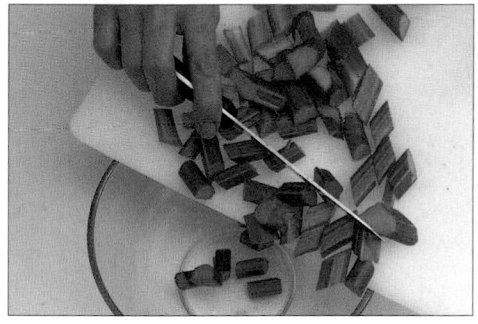

1 Preheat the oven to 200°C/400°F/ Gas 6. Chop the rhubarb into 2.5cm/1in pieces and put them in a bowl.

2 Add the mixed spice, orange rind and juice and sugar. Tip the rhubarb into a 1 litre/1¾ pint/4 cup pie dish.

NUTRITION NOTES

Per portion:
Energy	71Kcals/299kJ
Fat	2.5g
Saturated Fat	1.41g
Cholesterol	5.74mg
Fibre	1.48g

3 Melt the butter and brush it over the pastry. Lift the pastry on to the pie dish, butter-side up, and crumple it up decoratively to cover the pie.

> VARIATION
> Other fruit can be used in this pie – just prepare depending on type.

4 Put the dish on a baking sheet and bake for 20 minutes, until golden brown. Reduce the heat to 180°C/350°F/ Gas 4 and bake for a further 10–15 minutes, until the rhubarb is tender.

Blushing Pears

Pears poached in rosé wine and sweet spices absorb all the subtle flavours and turn a delightful soft pink colour.

Ingredients

Serves 6

6 firm eating pears
300ml/½ pint/1¼ cups rosé wine
150ml/¼ pint/⅔ cup cranberry or
* clear apple juice*
strip of thinly pared orange rind
1 cinnamon stick
4 whole cloves
1 bay leaf
75ml/5 tbsp caster sugar
small bay leaves, to decorate

1 Thinly peel the pears with a sharp knife or vegetable peeler, leaving the stalks attached.

2 Pour the wine and cranberry or apple juice into a large heavy-based saucepan. Add the orange rind, cinnamon stick, cloves, bay leaf and sugar.

3 Heat gently, stirring all the time, until the sugar has dissolved. Add the pears and stand them upright in the pan. Pour in enough cold water to barely cover them. Cover and cook gently for 20–30 minutes, or until just tender, turning and basting occasionally.

4 Using a slotted spoon, gently lift the pears out of the syrup and transfer to a serving dish.

5 Bring the syrup to the boil and boil rapidly for 10–15 minutes, or until it has reduced by half.

6 Strain the syrup and pour over the pears. Serve hot or well-chilled, decorated with small bay leaves.

Nutrition Notes

Per portion:

Energy	148Kcals/620kJ
Fat	0.16g
Saturated Fat	0
Fibre	2.93g

Cook's Tip

Check the pears by piercing with a skewer or sharp knife towards the end of the poaching time, because some may cook more quickly than others. Serve straight away, or leave to cool in the syrup and then chill.

COLD DESSERTS

There is such a vast range of ready-made desserts available today that it may hardly seem worth making your own, but it is definitely well worth the effort. In no time at all, you can make and enjoy a wide variety of nutritious low fat delicious cold desserts, such as Rhubarb and Orange Water-ice, Apple and Blackberry Terrine, Mandarins in Syrup and Raspberry Vacherin.

APRICOT DELICE

A fluffy mousse base with a layer of fruit jelly on top makes this dessert doubly delicious.

Serves 8
2 x 400g/14oz cans apricots in natural juice
60ml/4 tbsp sugar
25ml/5 tbsp lemon juice
25ml/5 tsp powdered gelatine
425g/15oz low fat ready-to-serve custard
150ml/¼ pint/⅔ cup Greek-style yogurt
1 apricot, sliced, and fresh mint sprig, to decorate
whipped cream, to decorate (optional)

NUTRITION NOTES

Per portion:

Energy	155Kcals/649kJ
Fat	0.63g
Saturated Fat	0.33g
Fibre	0.9g

COOK'S TIP

Use reduced fat Greek yogurt to cut calories and fat. Add the finely grated rind of 1 lemon to the mixture, for extra flavour. Peaches or pears are good alternatives to apricots.

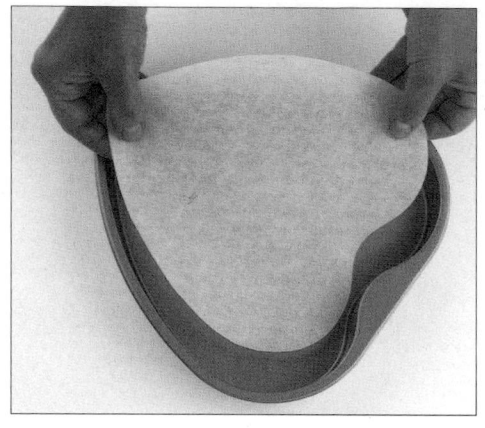

1 Line the base of a 1.2 litre/2 pint/5 cup heart-shaped or round cake tin with non-stick baking paper.

2 Drain the apricots, reserving the juice. Put the apricots in a food processor or blender fitted with a metal blade, together with the sugar and 60ml/4 tbsp of the apricot juice. Blend to a smooth purée.

3 Measure 30ml/2 tbsp of the apricot juice into a small bowl. Add the lemon juice, then sprinkle over 10ml/2 tsp of the gelatine. Leave for about 5 minutes, until spongy.

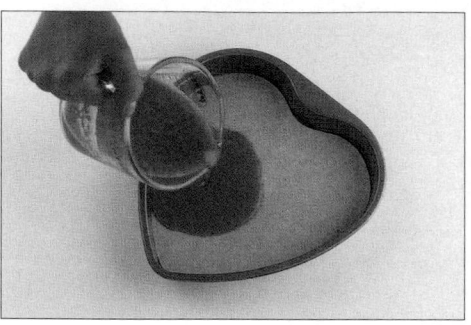

4 Stir the gelatine into half of the purée and pour into the prepared tin. Chill in the fridge for 1½ hours, or until firm.

5 Sprinkle the remaining 15ml/3 tsp of gelatine over 60ml/4 tbsp of the apricot juice. Leave for about 5 minutes until spongy. Mix the remaining apricot purée with the custard, yogurt and gelatine. Pour on to the layer of set fruit purée and chill for 3 hours.

6 Dip the cake tin into hot water for a few seconds and unmould the delice on to a serving plate and peel off the lining paper. Decorate with the sliced apricot and mint sprig; for a special occasion, pipe whipped cream round the edge.

MELON, GINGER AND GRAPEFRUIT

This pretty fruit combination is very light and refreshing for any summer meal.

INGREDIENTS

Serves 4

500g/1¼ lbs diced watermelon flesh
2 ruby or pink grapefruit
2 pieces stem ginger in syrup
30ml/2 tbsp stem ginger syrup

NUTRITION NOTES

Per portion:

Energy	76Kcals/324.5kJ
Fat	0.42g
Saturated Fat	0.125g
Cholesterol	0
Fibre	0.77g

1 Remove any seeds from the watermelon and discard. Cut the fruit into bite-size chunks. Set aside.

2 Using a small sharp knife, cut away all the peel and white pith from the grapefruits and carefully lift out the segments, catching any juice in a bowl.

3 Finely chop the stem ginger and put in a serving bowl with the melon cubes and grapefruit segments, also adding the juice.

4 Spoon over the ginger syrup and toss the fruits lightly to mix evenly. Chill before serving.

COOK'S TIP
Take care to toss the fruits gently – grapefruit segments will break up easily and the appearance of the dish will be spoiled.

MANGO AND GINGER CLOUDS

The sweet, perfumed flavour of ripe mango combines beautifully with ginger, and this low fat dessert makes the very most of them both.

— INGREDIENTS —

Serves 6
3 ripe mangoes
3 pieces stem ginger
45ml/3 tbsp stem ginger syrup
75g/3oz/¹/₂ cup silken tofu
3 egg whites
6 pistachio nuts, chopped

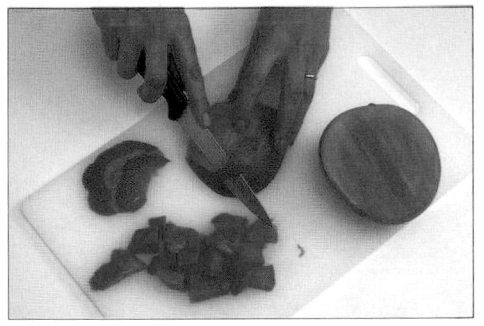

1 Cut the mangoes in half, remove the stones and peel. Roughly chop the mango flesh.

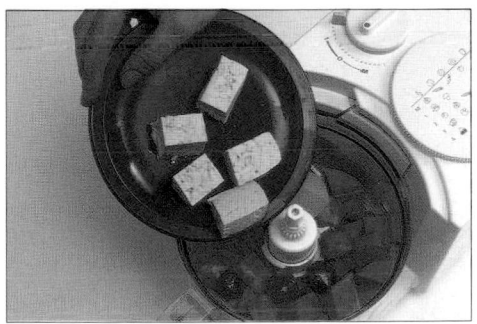

2 Put the chopped mango in a food processor bowl, with the ginger, syrup and tofu. Process the mixture until smooth and spoon into a mixing bowl.

3 Put the egg whites in a bowl and whisk them until they form soft peaks. Fold them lightly into the mango mixture.

4 Spoon the mixture into wide dishes or glasses and chill before serving, sprinkled with the chopped pistachios.

— NUTRITION NOTES —

Per portion:
Energy	112Kcals/472kJ
Fat	3.5g
Saturated Fat	0.52g
Cholesterol	0
Fibre	2.25g

COOK'S TIP
This dessert can be served lightly frozen. If you prefer not to use ginger, omit the ginger pieces and syrup and use 45ml/3 tbsp clear honey instead.

GOOSEBERRY CHEESE COOLER

1 Top and tail the gooseberries and place them in a pan. Finely grate the rind from the orange and squeeze out the juice, then add them both to the pan. Cover the pan and cook gently, stirring occasionally, until the fruit is tender.

2 Remove from the heat and stir in the honey. Purée the gooseberries with their juice in a blender or food processor until almost smooth. Cool.

3 Press the cottage cheese through a sieve until smooth. Stir half the cooled gooseberry purée into the cheese.

4 Spoon the cheese mixture into four serving glasses. Top each with gooseberry purée. Serve chilled.

COOK'S TIP
If fresh or frozen gooseberries are not available, canned ones are often packed in heavy syrup, so substitute a different fresh fruit.

MANGO AND LIME SORBET IN LIME SHELLS

This richly flavoured sorbet looks pretty served in the lime shells, but is also good served in scoops for a more traditional presentation.

INGREDIENTS

Serves 4
4 large limes
1 medium-size ripe mango
7.5ml/½ tsp powdered gelatine
2 egg whites
15ml/1 tbsp granulated sugar
lime rind strips, to decorate

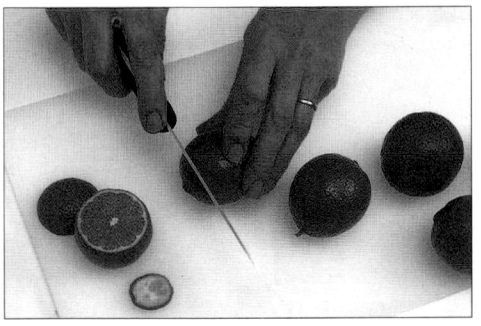

1 Cut a thick slice from the top of each of the limes, and then cut a thin slice from the bottom end so that the limes will stand upright. Squeeze out the juice, then use a small knife to remove all the white membrane from the centre.

2 Halve, stone, peel and chop the mango, then purée the flesh in a blender or food processor with 30ml/2 tbsp of the lime juice. Dissolve the gelatine in 45ml/3 tbsp of lime juice and stir it into the mango mixture.

3 Whisk the egg whites until they hold soft peaks. Whisk in the sugar, then quickly fold the egg-white mixture into the mango mixture. Spoon the sorbet into the lime shells. (Any leftover sorbet that will not fit in can be frozen in small ramekins.)

4 Wrap the shells in clear film and put in the freezer until the sorbet is firm. Before serving, allow the shells to stand at room temperature for about 10 minutes; decorate them with strips of lime rind.

COOK'S TIP
If you have any lime juice left over, it will freeze well for future use. Pour into a freezer container, seal and freeze for up to six months.

NUTRITION NOTES	
Per portion:	
Energy	50.5Kcals/215kJ
Fat	0.09g
Saturated Fat	0.3g
Cholesterol	0
Fibre	1g

APPLE AND BLACKBERRY TERRINE

Apples and blackberries are a classic autumn combination; they really complement each other. This pretty, three-layered terrine can be frozen, so you can enjoy it at any time of year.

INGREDIENTS

Serves 6
500g/1½lb cooking or eating apples
300ml/½ pint/1¼ cups sweet cider
15ml/1 tbsp clear honey
5ml/1 tsp vanilla essence
200g/7oz fresh or frozen and thawed
  blackberries
15ml/1 tbsp/1 sachet powdered gelatine
2 egg whites
apple slices and blackberries, to
  decorate

NUTRITION NOTES

Per portion:
Energy	72Kcals/306kJ
Fat	0.13g
Saturated Fat	0
Cholesterol	0
Fibre	2.1g

COOK'S TIP

For a quicker version, the mixture can be set without layering. Purée the apples and blackberries together, stir the dissolved gelatine and whisked egg whites into the mixture, turn the whole thing into the tin and leave the mixture to set.

1 Peel, core and chop the apples and place them in a saucepan, with half the cider. Bring the cider to the boil, and then cover the pan and let the apples simmer gently on a medium heat until tender.

2 Tip the apples into a blender or food processor and process them to a smooth purée. Stir in the honey and vanilla. Add half the blackberries to half the apple purée, and then process the mixture again until smooth. Sieve.

3 Heat the remaining cider until it is almost boiling, then sprinkle the powdered gelatine over and stir until the gelatine has completely dissolved. Add half the gelatine and cider liquid to the apple purée and half to the blackberry purée.

4 Leave the purées to cool until almost set. Whisk the egg whites until they are stiff, then quickly fold them into the apple purée. Remove half the purée to another bowl. Stir the remaining whole blackberries into half the apple purée, and then turn this into a 1.75 litre/3 pint/7½ cup loaf tin.

5 Top with the blackberry purée and spread it evenly. Finally, add a layer of the apple purée and smooth it evenly. To make sure the layers remain clearly separated, you can freeze each one until firm before adding the next.

6 Freeze until firm. To serve, allow to stand at room temperature for about 20 minutes to soften, then serve in thick slices, decorated with apples and blackberries.

QUICK APRICOT WHIP

INGREDIENTS

Serves 4

400g/14oz can apricot halves in juice
15ml/1 tbsp Grand Marnier or brandy
175g/6oz/³⁄₄ cup low fat yogurt
30ml/2 tsp flaked almonds

NUTRITION NOTES

Per portion:

Energy	114Kcals/480kJ
Fat	4.6g
Saturated Fat	0.57g
Cholesterol	0
Fibre	1.45g

1 Drain the juice from the apricots and place the fruit and liqueur in a blender or food processor.

2 Process the apricots until they are completely smooth.

3 Put alternate spoonfuls of the fruit purée and yogurt into four tall glasses or glass dishes, swirling them together slightly to give a marbled effect.

4 Lightly toast the almonds until they are golden-brown. Let them cool slightly and then sprinkle them on top of the desserts.

COOK'S TIP
If you prefer to omit the liqueur, add a little of the fruit juice from the can.

Mandarins in Syrup

Mandarins, tangerines, clementines, mineolas; any of these lovely citrus fruits are suitable for this recipe.

Ingredients

Serves 4
10 mandarin oranges
15ml/1 tbsp icing sugar
10ml/2 tsp orange-flower water
15ml/1 tbsp chopped pistachio nuts

1 Thinly pare a little of the rind from one mandarin and cut it into fine shreds for decoration. Squeeze the juice from two mandarins and set aside.

2 Peel the remaining fruit, removing as much of the white pith as possible. Arrange the peeled fruit whole in a wide dish.

3 Mix the mandarin juice, sugar and orange-flower water and pour it over the fruit. Cover the dish and chill for at least an hour.

4 Blanch the shreds of mandarin rind in boiling water for 30 seconds. Drain, leave to cool and then sprinkle them over the mandarins, with the pistachio nuts, to serve.

Nutrition Notes

Per portion:

Energy	53.25Kcals/223.5kJ
Fat	2.07g
Saturated Fat	0.28g
Cholesterol	0
Fibre	0.38g

Cook's Tip
Mandarin oranges look very attractive if you leave them whole, but you may prefer to separate the segments.

YOGURT SUNDAES WITH PASSION FRUIT

Here is a sundae you can enjoy every day! The frozen yogurt has less fat and fewer calories than traditional ice cream, and the fruits provide vitamins A and C.

INGREDIENTS

Serves 4
350g/12oz strawberries, hulled
* and halved*
2 passion fruit, halved
10ml/2 tsp icing sugar (optional)
2 ripe peaches, stoned and chopped
8 scoops (about 350g/12oz) vanilla or
* strawberry frozen yogurt*

> **COOK'S TIP**
> Choose reduced fat or virtually fat free frozen yogurt or ice cream, to cut the calories and fat.

1 Purée half the strawberries. Scoop out the passion fruit pulp and add it to the coulis. Sweeten, if necessary.

NUTRITION NOTES	
Per portion:	
Energy	135Kcals/560kJ
Fat	1g
Saturated Fat	0.5g
Cholesterol	3.5mg

2 Spoon half the remaining strawberries and half the chopped peaches into four tall sundae glasses. Top each dessert with a scoop of frozen yogurt. Set aside a few choice pieces of fruit for decoration, and use the rest to make a further layer on the top of each sundae. Top each sundae with a final scoop of frozen yogurt.

3 Pour over the passion fruit coulis and decorate the sundaes with the remaining strawberries and pieces of peach. Serve immediately.

FRUIT FONDUE WITH HAZELNUT DIP

INGREDIENTS

Serves 2
selection of fresh fruit for dipping, such
* as satsumas, kiwi fruit, grapes*
* and physalis (cape gooseberries)*
50g/2oz/¹⁄₂ cup reduced fat soft cheese
150ml/5fl oz/1¹⁄₄ cup low fat
* hazelnut yogurt*
5ml/1 tsp vanilla essence
5ml/1 tsp caster sugar

NUTRITION NOTES	
Per portion (dip only):	
Energy	170Kcals/714kJ
Fat	4g
Saturated Fat	2.5g
Cholesterol	6.5mg

1 First prepare the fruit. Peel and segment the satsumas, removing as much of the white pith as possible. Quarter the kiwi fruits, wash the grapes and peel back the papery casing on the physalis.

2 Beat the soft cheese with the yogurt, vanilla essence and sugar in a bowl. Spoon the mixture into a glass serving dish set on a platter or into small pots on individual plates.

3 Arrange the prepared fruits around the dip and serve immediately.

RASPBERRY VACHERIN

Meringue rounds filled with orange-flavoured low fat fromage frais and fresh raspberries make this a perfect dinner party dessert.

INGREDIENTS

Serves 6
3 egg whites
175g/6oz/³/4 cup caster sugar
5ml/1 tsp chopped almonds
icing sugar, for dusting
raspberry leaves, to decorate (optional)

For the filling
175g/6oz/³/4 cup low fat soft cheese
15–30ml/1–2 tbsp clear honey
15–30ml/1–2 tbsp Cointreau
120ml/4fl oz/¹/2 cup low fat
  fromage frais
225g/8oz raspberries

NUTRITION NOTES

Per portion:	
Energy	197Kcals/837.5kJ
Fat	1.02g
Saturated Fat	0.36g
Cholesterol	1.67mg
Fibre	1g

COOK'S TIP
When making the meringue, whisk the egg whites until they are so stiff that you can turn the bowl upside-down without them falling out.

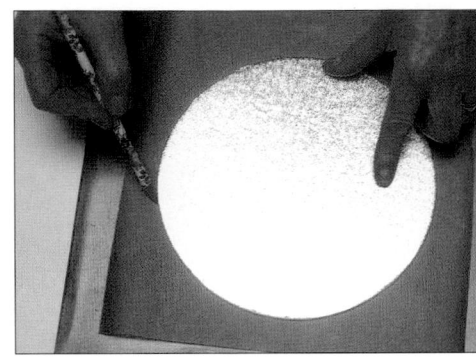

1 Preheat the oven to 140°C/275°F/ Gas 1. Draw a 20cm/8in circle on two pieces of non-stick baking paper. Turn the paper over so the marking is on the underside and use it to line two heavy baking sheets.

2 Whisk the egg whites in a clean bowl until very stiff, then gradually whisk in the caster sugar to make a stiff meringue mixture.

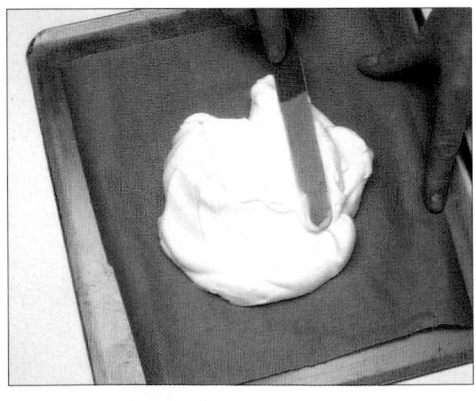

3 Spoon the mixture on to the circles on the prepared baking sheets, spreading the meringue evenly to the edges. Sprinkle one meringue round with the chopped almonds.

4 Bake for 1¹/2–2 hours until crisp and dry, and then carefully lift the meringue rounds off the baking sheets. Peel away the paper and cool the meringues on a wire rack.

5 To make the filling, cream the soft cheese with the honey and liqueur in a bowl. Gradually fold in the fromage frais and the raspberries, reserving three berries for decoration.

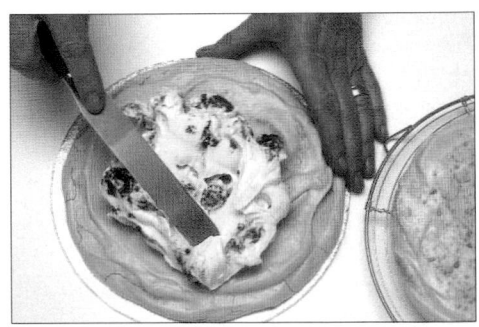

6 Place the plain meringue round on a board, spread with the filling and top with the nut-covered round. Dust with the icing sugar, transfer to a serving plate and decorate with the reserved raspberries and a sprig of raspberry leaves, if you like.

PRUNE AND ORANGE POTS

This simple, storecupboard dessert can be made in minutes. Serve straight away or, for the best result, chill it for about half an hour before serving.

INGREDIENTS

Serves 4

225g/8oz/1½ cups ready-to-eat dried prunes
150ml/¼ pint/⅔ cup orange juice
225g/8oz/1 cup low fat natural yogurt
shreds of orange rind, to decorate

NUTRITION NOTES

Per portion:

Energy	112Kcals/474kJ
Fat	0.62g
Saturated Fat	0.34g
Cholesterol	2.25mg
Fibre	2.8g

1 Remove the stones from the prunes and roughly chop them. Place them in a pan with the orange juice.

2 Bring the juice to the boil, stirring. Reduce the heat, cover and leave to simmer for 5 minutes, until the prunes are tender and the liquid has reduced by half.

3 Remove from the heat, allow to cool slightly and then beat well with a wooden spoon, until the fruit breaks down to a rough purée.

> ### COOK'S TIP
> This dessert can also be made with other ready-to-eat dried fruit, such as apricots or peaches. For a special occasion, add a dash of brandy or Cointreau with the yogurt.

4 Transfer the purée mixture to a bowl. Stir in the low fat yogurt, swirling the yogurt and fruit purée together lightly to give an attractive marbled effect.

5 Spoon the mixture into individual dishes or stemmed glasses, smoothing the tops.

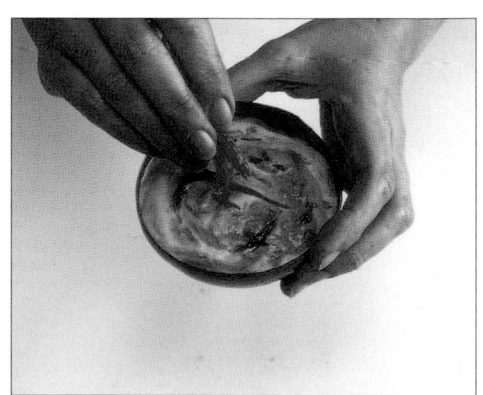

6 Top each pot with a few shreds of orange rind, to decorate. Chill before serving.

TROPICAL FOAMY YOGURT RING

An impressive, light and colourful tropical dessert with a truly fruity flavour.

─── **INGREDIENTS** ───

Serves 6
For the yogurt ring
175ml/6fl oz/³⁄4 cup tropical fruit juice
15ml/1 tbsp/1 sachet powdered gelatine
3 egg whites
150g/5oz low fat natural yogurt
finely grated rind of 1 lime

For the filling
1 mango
2 kiwi fruit
10–12 physalis cape gooseberries
juice of 1 lime

1 Place the tropical fruit juice in a small pan and sprinkle the powdered gelatine over. Heat gently until the gelatine has dissolved.

2 Whisk the egg whites in a clean, dry bowl until they hold soft peaks. Continue whisking hard, while gradually adding the yogurt and lime rind.

3 Continue whisking hard and pour in the hot gelatine and the egg white and yogurt mixture in a steady stream, until everything is smooth and evenly mixed.

4 Quickly pour the mixture into a 1.5 litre/2½ pint/6¼ cup ring mould. Chill the mould in the fridge until set. The mixture will separate into two layers.

5 Halve, stone, peel and dice the mango. Peel and slice the kiwi fruit. Remove the outer leaves from the physalis and cut in half. Toss all the fruits together and stir in the lime juice.

6 Run a knife around the edge of the ring to loosen the mixture. Dip the tin quickly into cold water and then turn the chilled yogurt mould out on to a serving plate. Spoon all the prepared fruit into the centre of the ring and serve immediately.

─── **NUTRITION NOTES** ───

Per portion:
Energy	83.5Kcals/355kJ
Fat	0.67g
Saturated Fat	0.27g
Cholesterol	2.16mg
Fibre	1.77g

COOK'S TIP
Any mixture of fruit works in this recipe, depending on the season. In summer try using apple juice in the ring mixture and fill it with luscious, red summer fruits.

Strawberry Rose-petal Pashka

This lighter version of a tradi-tional Russian dessert is ideal for dinner parties – make it a day or two in advance for best results.

Ingredients

Serves 4
350g/12oz/1½ cups cottage cheese
175g/6oz/¾ cup low fat natural yogurt
30ml/2 tbsp clear honey
2.5ml/½ tsp rose-water
275g/10oz strawberries
handful of scented pink rose petals,
    to decorate

Nutrition Notes

Per portion:
Energy	150.5Kcals/634kJ
Fat	3.83g
Saturated Fat	2.32g
Cholesterol	0.13mg
Fibre	0.75g

Cook's Tip
The flowerpot shape is traditional for pashka, but you could make it in any shape – the small porcelain heart-shaped moulds with drain-ing holes usually reserved for *coeurs à la crème* make a pretty alternative.

1 Drain any free liquid from the cottage cheese and tip the cheese into a sieve. Use a wooden spoon to rub it through the sieve into a bowl.

2 Stir the yogurt, honey and rose-water into the cheese.

3 Roughly chop about half the straw-berries and stir them into the cheese mixture.

4 Line a new, clean flowerpot or a sieve with muslin and tip the cheese mixture in. Leave it to drain over a bowl for several hours, or overnight.

5 Invert the flowerpot or sieve on to a serving plate, turn out the pashka and remove the muslin.

6 Decorate the pashka with strawber-ries and rose petals. Serve chilled.

CAKES AND BAKES

We tend to think of cakes and bakes being out of bounds for those following a low fat diet, but you will be pleased to learn that this is not the case at all. There are many ways of creating delicious cakes and bakes without the need for high fat mixtures, and all the cakes and bakes in this chapter, both sweet and savoury, are low in fat. Choose from tempting recipes for such delights as Tia Maria Gâteau, Coffee Sponge Drops, Muscovado Meringues, and Chocolate and Banana Brownies.

TIA MARIA GÂTEAU

A feather-light coffee sponge with a creamy liqueur-flavoured filling.

INGREDIENTS

Serves 8
75g/3oz/³/₄ cup plain flour
30ml/2 tbsp instant coffee powder
3 eggs
115g/4oz/¹/₂ cup caster sugar
coffee beans, to decorate (optional)

For the filling
175g/6oz/³/₄ cup low fat soft cheese
15ml/1 tbsp clear honey
15ml/1 tbsp Tia Maria liqueur
50g/2oz/¹/₄ cup stem ginger,
  roughly chopped

For the icing
225g/8oz/1³/₄ cups icing sugar, sifted
10ml/2 tsp coffee essence
15ml/1 tbsp water
5ml/1 tsp reduced fat cocoa powder

NUTRITION NOTES

Per portion:
Energy	226Kcals/951kJ
Fat	3.14g
Saturated Fat	1.17g
Cholesterol	75.03mg
Fibre	0.64g

COOK'S TIP
When folding in the flour mixture in step 3, be careful not to remove the air, as it helps the cake to rise.

1 Preheat the oven to 190°C/375°F/ Gas 5. Grease and line a 20cm/8in deep round cake tin. Sift the flour and coffee powder together on to a sheet of greaseproof paper.

2 Whisk the eggs and sugar in a bowl with a hand-held electric whisk until thick and mousse-like. (When the whisk is lifted, a trail should remain on the surface of the mixture for at least 15 seconds.)

3 Gently fold in the flour mixture with a metal spoon. Turn the mixture into the prepared tin. Bake the sponge for 30–35 minutes or until it springs back when lightly pressed. Turn on to a wire rack to cool completely.

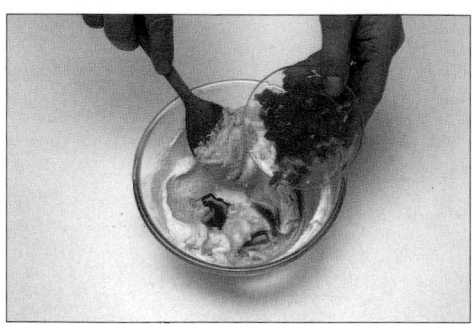

4 To make the filling, mix the soft cheese with the honey in a bowl. Beat until smooth, then stir in the Tia Maria and chopped stem ginger.

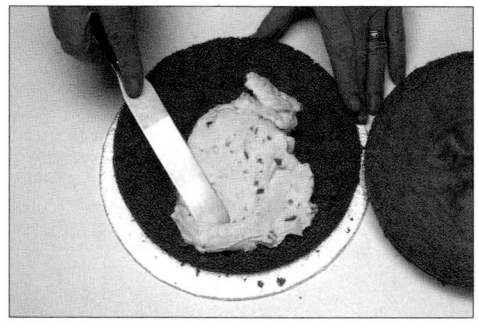

5 Split the cake in half horizontally and sandwich the two halves together with the Tia Maria filling.

6 Make the icing. In a bowl, mix the icing sugar and coffee essence with enough water to make a consistency that will coat the back of a wooden spoon. Pour three-quarters of the icing over the cake, spreading it evenly to the edges. Stir the cocoa into the remaining icing until smooth. Spoon into a piping bag fitted with a writing nozzle and pipe the mocha icing over the coffee icing. Decorate with coffee beans, if liked.

CHOCOLATE AND ORANGE ANGEL CAKE

This light-as-air sponge with its fluffy icing is virtually fat free, yet tastes heavenly.

— INGREDIENTS —

Serves 10
25g/1oz/¹/₄ cup plain flour
15g/¹/₂oz/2 tbsp reduced fat
   cocoa powder
15g/¹/₂oz/2 tbsp cornflour
pinch of salt
5 egg whites
2.5ml/¹/₂ tsp cream of tartar
115g/4oz/scant ¹/₂ cup caster sugar
blanched and shredded rind of
   1 orange, to decorate

For the icing
200g/7oz/1 cup caster sugar
1 egg white

— NUTRITION NOTES —

Per portion:
Energy	53Kcals/644kJ
Fat	0.27g
Saturated Fat	0.13g
Fibre	0.25g

COOK'S TIP
Make sure you do not over-beat the egg whites. They should not be stiff but should form soft peaks, so that the air bubbles can expand further during cooking and help the cake to rise.

1 Preheat the oven to 180°C/350°F/ Gas 4. Sift the flour, cocoa powder, cornflour and salt together three times. Beat the egg whites in a large clean, dry bowl until foamy. Add the cream of tartar, then whisk until soft peaks form.

2 Add the caster sugar to the egg whites a spoonful at a time, whisking after each addition. Sift a third of the flour and cocoa mixture over the meringue and gently fold in. Repeat, sifting and folding in the flour and cocoa mixture two more times.

3 Spoon the mixture into a non-stick 20cm/8in ring mould and level the top. Bake for 35 minutes or until springy to the touch. Turn upside-down on to a wire rack and leave to cool in the tin. Carefully ease out of the tin.

4 For the icing, put the sugar in a pan with 75ml/5 tbsp cold water. Stir over a low heat until dissolved. Boil until the syrup reaches a temperature of 120°C/240°F on a sugar thermometer, or when a drop of the syrup makes a soft ball when dropped into a cup of cold water. Remove from the heat.

5 Whisk the egg white until stiff. Add the syrup in a thin stream, whisking all the time. Continue to whisk until the mixture is very thick and fluffy.

6 Spread the icing over the top and sides of the cooled cake. Sprinkle the orange rind over the top of the cake and serve.

CINNAMON APPLE GÂTEAU

Make this lovely cake for an autumn celebration.

INGREDIENTS

Serves 8
3 eggs
115g/4oz/½ cup caster sugar
75g/3oz/¾ cup plain flour
5ml/1 tsp ground cinnamon

For the filling and topping
4 large eating apples
60ml/4 tbsp clear honey
15ml/ 1 tbsp water
75g/3oz/½ cup sultanas
2.5ml/½ tsp ground cinnamon
350g/12oz/1½ cups low fat soft cheese
60ml/4 tbsp reduced fat fromage frais
10ml/2 tsp lemon juice
45ml/3 tbsp apricot glaze
mint sprig, to decorate

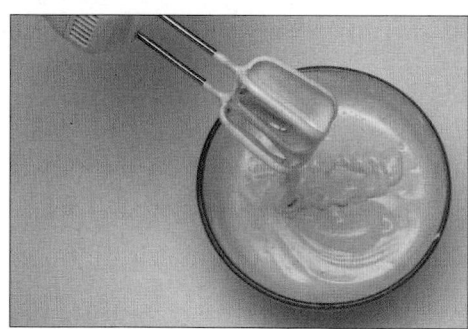

1 Preheat the oven to 190°C/375°F/ Gas 5. Grease and line a 23cm/9in sandwich cake tin. Place the eggs and caster sugar in a bowl and beat with a hand-held electric whisk until thick and mousse-like. (When the whisk is lifted, a trail should remain on the surface of the mixture for at least 15 seconds.)

NUTRITION NOTES	
Per portion:	
Energy	244 Kcals/1023kJ
Fat	4.05g
Saturated Fat	1.71g
Cholesterol	77.95mg
Fibre	1.50g

2 Sift the flour and cinnamon over the egg mixture and fold in with a large spoon. Pour into the prepared tin and bake for 25–30 minutes or until the cake springs back when lightly pressed. Turn the cake on to a wire rack to cool.

3 To make the filling, peel, core and slice three of the apples and put them in a saucepan. Add 30ml/2 tbsp of the honey and the water. Cover and cook over a gentle heat for about 10 minutes. Add the sultanas and cinnamon, stir well, replace the lid and leave to cool.

4 Put the soft cheese in a bowl with the remaining honey, the fromage frais and half the lemon juice. Beat until the mixture is smooth.

5 Halve the cake horizontally, place the bottom half on a board and drizzle over any liquid from the apples. Spread with two-thirds of the cheese mixture, then top with the apple filling. Fit the top of the cake in place.

6 Swirl the remaining cheese mixture over the top of the sponge. Core and slice the remaining apple, sprinkle with lemon juice and use to decorate the edge of the cake. Brush the apple with the apricot glaze and place mint sprigs on top, to decorate.

COOK'S TIP
Apricot glaze is useful for brushing over any kind of fresh fruit topping or filling. Place a few spoonfuls of apricot jam in a small pan along with a squeeze of lemon juice. Heat the jam, stirring until it is melted and runny. Pour the melted jam into a wire sieve set over a bowl. Stir the jam with a wooden spoon to help it go through. Return the strained jam to the pan. Keep the glaze warm until needed.

COFFEE SPONGE DROPS

These are delicious on their own, but taste even better with a filling made by mixing low fat soft cheese with drained and chopped stem ginger.

INGREDIENTS

Makes 12
50g/2oz/½ cup plain flour
15ml/1 tbsp instant coffee powder
2 eggs
75g/3oz/6 tbsp caster sugar

For the filling
115g/4oz/½ cup low fat soft cheese
40g/1½oz/¼ cup chopped
  stem ginger

COOK'S TIP
As an alternative to stem ginger in the filling, try walnuts.

1 Preheat the oven to 190°C/375°F/ Gas 5. Line two baking sheets with non-stick baking paper. Make the filling by beating together the soft cheese and stem ginger. Chill until required. Sift the flour and instant coffee powder together.

NUTRITION NOTES

Per portion:
Energy	69Kcals/290kJ
Fat	1.36g
Saturated Fat	0.50g
Cholesterol	33.33mg
Fibre	0.29g

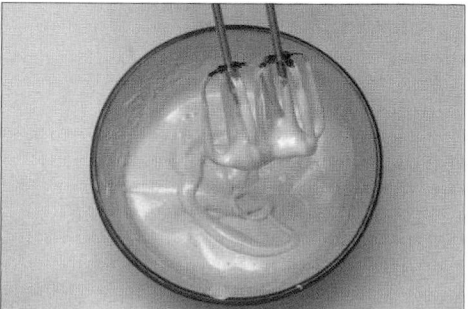

2 Combine the eggs and caster sugar in a bowl. Beat with a hand-held electric whisk until thick and mousse-like. (When the whisk is lifted, a trail should remain on the surface of the mixture for at least 15 seconds.)

3 Carefully add the sifted flour and coffee mixture and gently fold in with a metal spoon, being careful not to knock out any air.

4 Spoon the mixture into a piping bag fitted with a 1cm/½in plain nozzle. Pipe 4cm/1½in rounds on the baking sheets. Bake for 12 minutes. Cool on a wire rack, then sandwich together with the filling.

CHOCOLATE AND BANANA BROWNIES

Nuts traditionally give brownies their chewy texture. Here oat bran is used instead, creating a low fat, moist, moreish, yet healthy alternative.

INGREDIENTS

Serves 9

75ml/5 tbsp reduced fat cocoa powder
15ml/1 tbsp caster sugar
75ml/5 tbsp skimmed milk
3 large bananas, mashed
215g/7½oz/1 cup soft light brown sugar
5ml/1 tsp vanilla essence
5 egg whites
75g/3oz/¾ cup self-raising flour
75g/3oz/¾ cup oat bran
15ml/1 tbsp icing sugar, for dusting

NUTRITION NOTES

Per portion:
Energy	230Kcals/968kJ
Fat	2.15g
Saturated Fat	0.91g
Fibre	1.89g

COOK'S TIPS
Store these brownies in an airtight tin for a day before eating – they improve with keeping.

You'll find reduced fat cocoa powder in health food stores. If you can't find it, ordinary cocoa powder will work just as well, but, of course, the fat content will be much higher!

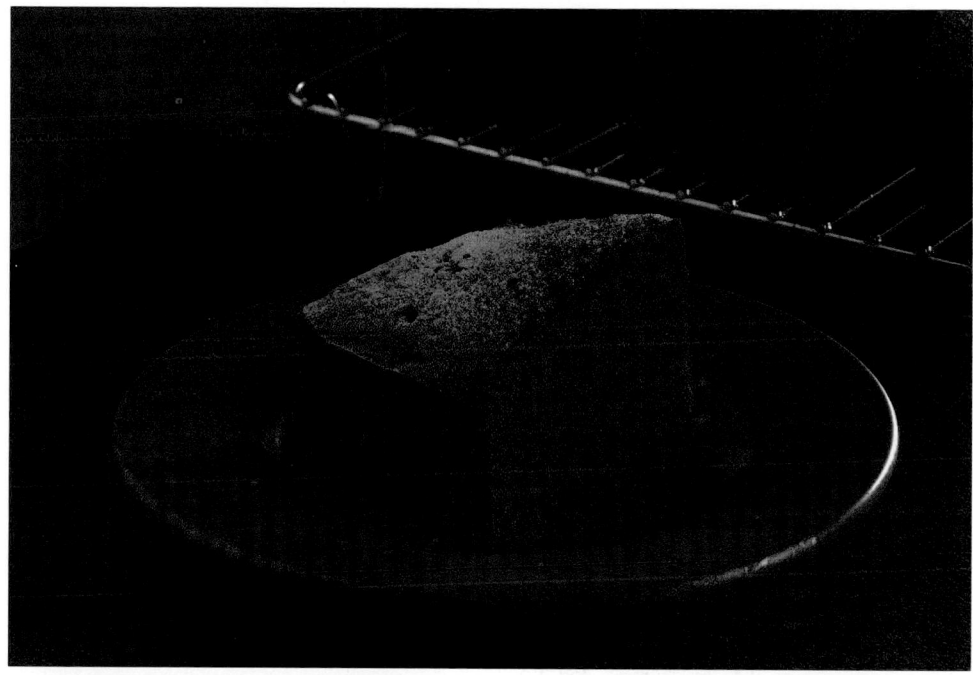

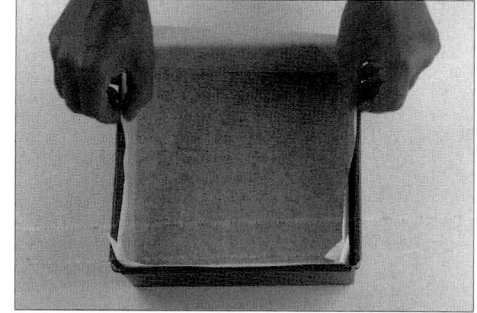

1 Preheat the oven to 180°C/350°F/ Gas 4. Line a 20cm/8in square tin with non-stick baking paper.

2 Blend the reduced fat cocoa powder and caster sugar with the skimmed milk. Add the bananas, soft light brown sugar and vanilla essence.

3 Lightly beat the egg whites with a fork. Add the chocolate mixture and continue to beat well. Sift the flour over the mixture and fold in with the oat bran. Pour into the prepared tin.

4 Cook in the preheated oven for 40 minutes or until firm. Cool in the tin for 10 minutes, then turn out on to a wire rack. Cut into squares and lightly dust with icing sugar before serving.

PEACH SWISS ROLL

A feather-light sponge enclosing peach jam – delicious at tea time.

INGREDIENTS

Serves 6–8
3 eggs
115g/4oz/¹/₂ cup caster sugar
75g/3oz/³/₄ cup plain flour, sifted
15ml/1 tbsp boiling water
90ml/6 tbsp peach jam
icing sugar, for dusting (optional)

NUTRITION NOTES

Per portion:

Energy	178Kcals/746kJ
Fat	2.45g
Saturated Fat	0.67g
Cholesterol	82.50mg
Fibre	0.33g

COOK'S TIP
To decorate the Swiss roll with glacé icing, put 115g/4oz glacé icing in a piping bag fitted with a small writing nozzle and pipe lines over the top.

1 Preheat the oven to 200°C/400°F/ Gas 6. Grease a 30 x 20cm/12 x 8in Swiss roll tin and line with non-stick baking paper. Combine the eggs and sugar in a bowl. Beat with a hand-held electric whisk until thick and mousse-like. (When the whisk is lifted, a trail should remain on the surface of the mixture for at least 15 seconds.)

2 Carefully fold in the flour with a large metal spoon, then add the boiling water in the same way.

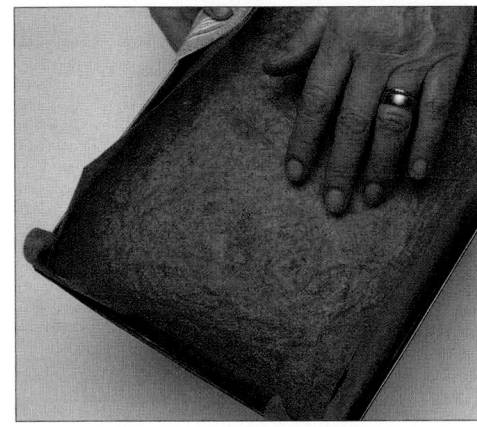

3 Spoon into the prepared tin, spread evenly to the edges and bake for about 10–12 minutes until the cake springs back when lightly pressed.

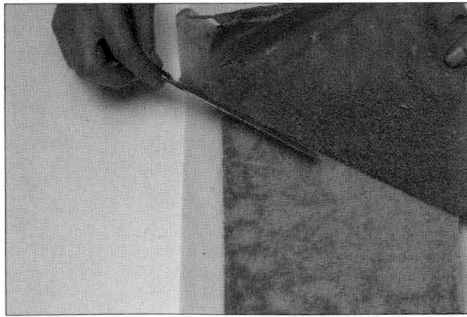

4 Spread a sheet of greaseproof paper on a flat surface, sprinkle it with caster sugar, then invert the cake on top. Peel off the lining paper.

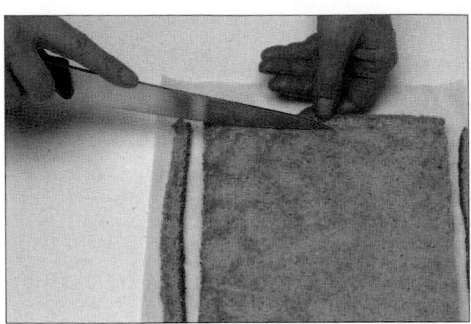

5 Neatly trim the edges of the cake. Make a neat cut two-thirds of the way through the cake, about 1cm/¹/₂in from the short edge nearest you.

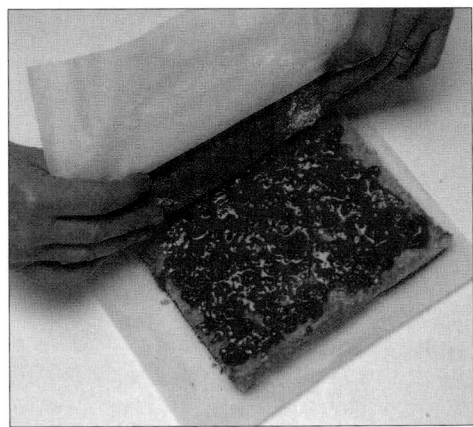

6 Spread the cake with the peach jam and roll up quickly from the partially cut end. Hold in position for a minute, making sure the join is underneath. Cool on a wire rack. Decorate with glacé icing (see Cook's Tip) or dust with icing sugar before serving.

LEMON CHIFFON CAKE

Lemon mousse provides a tangy filling for this light lemon sponge.

INGREDIENTS

Serves 8
2 eggs
75g/3oz/6 tbsp caster sugar
grated rind of 1 lemon
50g/2oz/½ cup sifted plain flour
lemon shreds, to decorate

For the filling
2 eggs, separated
75g/3oz/6 tbsp caster sugar
grated rind and juice of 1 lemon
30ml/2 tbsp water
15ml/1 tbsp gelatine
125ml/4fl oz/½ cup low fat
   fromage frais

For the icing
15ml/1 tbsp lemon juice
115g/4oz/scant 1 cup icing sugar, sifted

1 Preheat the oven to 180°C/350°F/ Gas 4. Grease and line a 20cm/8in loose-bottomed cake tin. Whisk the eggs, sugar and lemon rind together with a hand-held electric whisk until thick and mousse-like. Gently fold in the flour, then turn the mixture into the prepared tin.

2 Bake for 20–25 minutes until the cake springs back when lightly pressed in the centre. Turn on to a wire rack to cool. Once cold, split the cake in half horizontally and return the lower half to the clean cake tin.

3 Make the filling. Put the egg yolks, sugar, lemon rind and juice in a bowl. Beat with a hand-held electric whisk until thick, pale and creamy.

4 Pour the water into a heat-proof bowl and sprinkle the gelatine on top. Leave until spongy, then stir over simmering water until dissolved. Cool, then whisk into the yolk mixture. Fold in the fromage frais. When the mixture begins to set, whisk the egg whites to soft peaks. Fold the egg whites into the mousse mixture.

5 Pour the lemon mousse over the sponge in the cake tin, spreading it to the edges. Set the second layer of sponge on top and chill until set.

6 Slide a palette knife dipped in hot water between the tin and the cake to loosen it, then carefully transfer the cake to a serving plate. Make the icing by adding enough lemon juice to the icing sugar to make a mixture thick enough to coat the back of a wooden spoon. Pour over the cake and spread evenly to the edges. Decorate with the lemon shreds.

NUTRITION NOTES

Per portion:
Energy	202Kcals/849kJ
Fat	2.81g
Saturated Fat	0.79g
Cholesterol	96.41mg
Fibre	0.20g

COOK'S TIP
The mousse should be just setting when the egg whites are added. Speed up this process by placing the bowl of mousse in iced water.

BANANA AND GINGERBREAD SLICES

Very quick to make and
deliciously moist due to the
addition of bananas.

INGREDIENTS

Makes 20
275g/10oz/2 cups plain flour
20ml/4 tsp ground ginger
10ml/2 tsp mixed spice
5ml/1 tsp bicarbonate of soda
115g/4oz/¹/2 cup soft light brown sugar
60ml/4 tbsp sunflower oil
30ml/2 tbsp molasses or black treacle
30ml/2 tbsp malt extract
2 eggs
60ml/4 tbsp orange juice
3 bananas
115g/4oz/²/3 cup raisins

NUTRITION NOTES
Per portion:	
Energy	148Kcals/621kJ
Fat	3.07g
Saturated Fat	0.53g
Cholesterol	19.30mg
Fibre	0.79g

VARIATION
To make Spiced Honey and
Banana Cake: omit the ground
ginger and add another 5ml/1 tsp
mixed spice; omit the malt extract
and the molasses or treacle and
add 60ml/4 tbsp strong-flavoured
clear honey instead; and replace
the raisins with either sultanas, or
coarsely chopped ready-to-eat
dried apricots, or semi-dried
pineapple. If you choose to use
the pineapple, then you could also
replace the orange juice with fresh
pineapple juice.

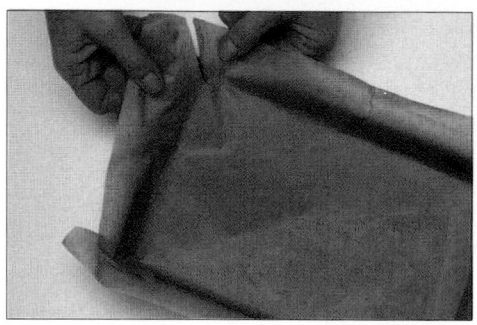

1 Preheat the oven to 180°C/350°F/
Gas 4. Lightly grease and line an
18 x 28cm/7 x 11in baking tin.

2 Sift the flour into a bowl with the
spices and bicarbonate of soda. Mix
in the sugar with some of the flour and
sift it all into the bowl.

3 Make a well in the centre, add the
oil, molasses or black treacle, malt
extract, eggs and orange juice and mix
together thoroughly.

4 Mash the bananas, add them to
the bowl with the raisins and mix
well together.

5 Pour the mixture into the prepared
tin and bake for about 35–40
minutes, until the centre springs back
when lightly pressed.

6 Leave the cake in the tin to cool for
5 minutes, then turn out on to a
wire rack and leave to cool completely.
Cut into 20 slices.

COOK'S TIP
The flavour of this cake develops
as it keeps, so if you can, store it
for a few days before eating.

SCONES, MUFFINS, BUNS AND BISCUITS

Many scones, muffins, buns and biscuits are low in fat and make ideal snacks or treats at any time of day. Try serving them on their own or with a little low fat spread, honey or jam. They are delicious served warm for breakfast or brunch, cold for afternoon tea or packed up and taken away, to enjoy at your leisure. We include a selection of tempting scones, muffins, buns and biscuits, including Pineapple and Cinnamon Drop Scones, Date and Apple Muffins, Banana and Apricot Chelsea Buns and Oaty Crisps.

PINEAPPLE AND CINNAMON DROP SCONES

Making the batter with pineapple juice instead of milk cuts down on fat and adds to the taste.

INGREDIENTS

Makes 24
*115g/4oz/1 cup self-raising wholemeal
   flour*
115g/4oz/1 cup self-raising white flour
5ml/1 tsp ground cinnamon
15ml/1 tbsp caster sugar
1 egg
300ml/½ pint/1¼ cups pineapple juice
*75g/3oz/½ cup semi-dried pineapple,
   chopped*

NUTRITION NOTES

Per portion:
Energy	15Kcals/215kJ
Fat	0.81g
Saturated Fat	0.14g
Cholesterol	8.02mg
Fibre	0.76g

1 Preheat a griddle, heavy-based frying pan or an electric frying pan. Put the wholemeal flour in a mixing bowl. Sift in the white flour, add the cinnamon and sugar and make a well in the centre.

COOK'S TIP
Drop scones do not keep well and are best eaten freshly cooked. Other semi-dried fruit, such as apricots or pears, can be used in place of the pineapple.

2 Add the egg with half the pineapple juice and gradually incorporate the surrounding flour to make a smooth batter. Beat in the remaining juice with the chopped pineapple.

3 Lightly grease the griddle or pan. Drop tablespoons of the batter on to the surface, leaving them until they bubble and the bubbles begin to burst.

4 Turn the drop scones with a palette knife and cook until the underside is golden brown. Keep the cooked scones warm and moist by wrapping them in a clean napkin while continuing to cook successive batches.

DROP SCONES

These little scones are delicious spread with jam.

INGREDIENTS

Makes 18
225g/8oz/2 cups self-raising flour
2.5ml/¹/₂ tsp salt
15ml/1 tbsp caster sugar
1 egg, beaten
300ml/¹/₂ pint/1¹/₄ cups skimmed milk
oil, for frying

1 Preheat a griddle, heavy-based frying pan or an electric frying pan. Sift the flour and salt into a mixing bowl. Stir in the sugar and make a well in the centre.

2 Add the egg and half the milk, then gradually incorporate the surrounding flour to make a smooth batter. Beat in the remaining milk.

3 Lightly oil the griddle or pan. Drop tablespoons of the batter on to the surface, leaving them until they bubble and the bubbles begin to burst.

NUTRITION NOTES

Per portion:
Energy	64Kcals/270kJ
Fat	1.09g
Saturated Fat	0.2g
Cholesterol	11.03mg
Fibre	0.43g

4 Turn the drop scones over with a palette knife and cook until the underside is golden brown. Keep the cooked drop scones warm and moist by wrapping them in a clean napkin while cooking successive batches.

COOK'S TIP
For savoury scones, add 2 chopped spring onions and 15ml/1 tbsp of freshly grated Parmesan cheese. Serve with cottage cheese.

CHIVE AND POTATO SCONES

These little scones should be fairly thin, soft and crisp on the outside. They're extremely quick to make, so serve them for breakfast or lunch.

INGREDIENTS

Makes 20
450g/1lb potatoes
115g/4oz/1 cup plain flour, sifted
30ml/2 tbsp olive oil
30ml/2 tbsp snipped chives
salt and black pepper
low fat spread, for topping (optional)

NUTRITION NOTES

Per portion:
Energy	50Kcals/211kJ
Fat	1.24g
Saturated Fat	0.17g
Cholesterol	0
Fibre	0.54g

1 Cook the potatoes in a saucepan of boiling salted water for 20 minutes, then drain thoroughly. Return the potatoes to the clean pan and mash them. Preheat a griddle or heavy-based frying pan over a low heat.

COOK'S TIP
Cook the scones over a low heat so that the outsides do not burn before the insides are cooked through.

2 Add the flour, olive oil and snipped chives with a little salt and pepper to the hot mashed potato in the pan. Mix to a soft dough.

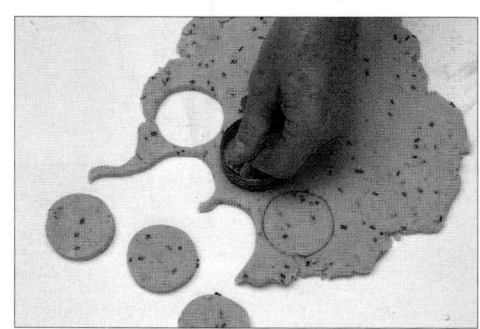

3 Roll out the dough on a well-floured surface to a thickness of 5mm/¼in and stamp out rounds with a 5cm/2in plain pastry cutter.

4 Cook the scones, in batches, on the hot griddle or frying pan for about 10 minutes until they are golden brown on both sides. Keep the heat low. Top with a little low fat spread, if you like, and serve immediately.

CHEESE AND CHIVE SCONES

Makes 9

115g/4oz/1 cup self-raising flour
150g/5oz/1 cup self-raising wholemeal
  flour
2.5ml/½ tsp salt
75g/3oz feta cheese
15ml/1 tbsp snipped fresh chives
150ml/¼ pint/⅔ cup skimmed milk,
  plus extra for glazing
1.25ml/¼ tsp cayenne pepper

1 Preheat the oven to 200°C/400°F/ Gas 6. Sift the flours and salt into a mixing bowl, adding any bran left over from the flour in the sieve.

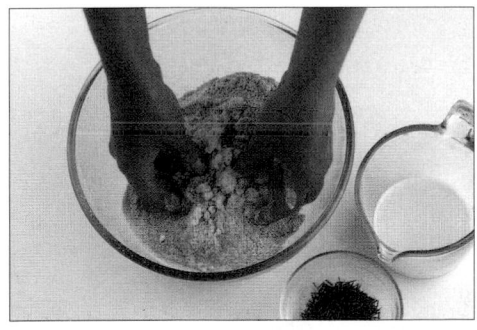

2 Crumble the feta cheese and rub into the dry ingredients. Stir in the chives, then add the milk and mix to a soft dough.

3 Turn out on to a floured surface and knead lightly until smooth. Roll out to 2cm/¾in thick and stamp out nine scones with a 6cm/2½in biscuit cutter.

4 Transfer the scones to a non-stick baking sheet. Brush with skimmed milk, then sprinkle over the cayenne pepper. Bake in the oven for 15 minutes, or until golden brown.

HAM AND TOMATO SCONES

These scones make an ideal accompaniment for soup. Choose a strongly flavoured ham, trimmed of fat, and chop it fairly finely, so that a little goes a long way. Use wholemeal flour or a mixture of wholemeal and white flour for extra flavour, texture and fibre.

INGREDIENTS

Makes 12

225g/8oz/2 cups self-raising flour
5ml/1 tsp dry mustard
5ml/1 tsp paprika, plus extra for
  sprinkling
2.5ml/½ tsp salt
25g/1oz/2 tbsp soft margarine
15ml/1 tbsp snipped fresh basil
50g/2oz/1 cup drained sun-dried
  tomatoes in oil, chopped
50g/2oz cooked ham, chopped
90–120ml/3–4fl oz/6 tbsp–½ cup
  skimmed milk, plus extra for brushing

1 Preheat the oven to 200°C/ 400°F/Gas 6. Flour a large baking sheet. Sift the flour, mustard, paprika and salt into a bowl. Rub in the margarine until the mixture resembles breadcrumbs.

NUTRITION NOTES

Per portion:	
Energy	113Kcals/474kJ
Fat	4.23g
Saturated Fat	0.65g
Cholesterol	2.98mg
Fibre	0.65g

2 Stir in the basil, sun-dried tomatoes and ham, and mix lightly. Pour in enough milk to mix to a soft dough.

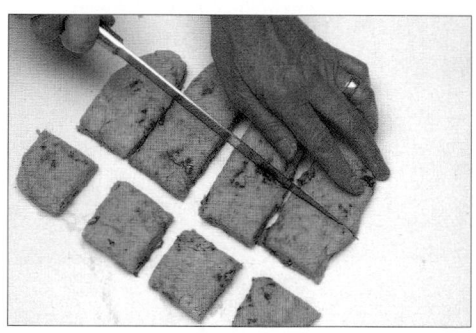

3 Turn the dough out on to a lightly floured surface, knead briefly and roll out to a 20 x 15cm/8 x 6in rectangle. Cut into 5cm/2in squares and arrange on the baking sheet.

4 Brush lightly with milk, sprinkle with paprika and bake for about 12–15 minutes. Transfer to a wire rack to cool.

COOK'S TIP
To cut calories and fat, choose dry-packed sun-dried tomatoes and soak them in warm water.

DATE AND APPLE MUFFINS

You will only need one or two of these wholesome muffins per person, as they are very filling.

INGREDIENTS

Makes 12
*150g/5oz/1¼ cups self-raising
    wholemeal flour*
*150g/5oz/1¼ cups self-raising
    white flour*
5ml/1 tsp ground cinnamon
5ml/1 tsp baking powder
25g/1 oz/2 tbsp soft margarine
75g/3oz/½ cup light muscovado sugar
1 eating apple
250ml/8fl oz/1 cup apple juice
30ml/2 tbsp pear and apple spread
1 egg, lightly beaten
75g/3oz/½ cup chopped dates
15ml/1 tbsp chopped pecan nuts

1 Preheat the oven to 200°C/400°F/ Gas 6. Arrange 12 paper cake cases in a deep muffin tin. Put the wholemeal flour in a mixing bowl. Sift in the white flour with the cinnamon and baking powder. Rub in the margarine until the mixture resembles breadcrumbs, then stir in the muscovado sugar.

2 Quarter and core the apple, chop the flesh finely and set aside. Stir a little of the apple juice with the pear and apple spread until smooth. Mix in the remaining juice, then add to the rubbed-in mixture with the egg. Add the chopped apple to the bowl with the dates. Mix quickly until just combined.

3 Divide the mixture among the muffin cases.

4 Sprinkle with the chopped pecan nuts. Bake the muffins for 20–25 minutes until golden brown and firm in the middle. Remove to a wire rack and serve while still warm.

NUTRITION NOTES

Per muffin:	
Energy	163Kcals/686kJ
Fat	2.98g
Saturated Fat	0.47g
Cholesterol	16.04mg
Fibre	1.97g

COOK'S TIP
Use a pear in place of the eating apple and chopped ready-to-eat dried apricots in place of the dates. Ground mixed spice is a good alternative to cinnamon.

RASPBERRY MUFFINS

These American muffins are made using baking powder and low fat buttermilk, giving them a light and spongy texture. They are delicious to eat at any time of the day.

INGREDIENTS

Makes 10–12
275g/10oz/2½ cups plain flour
15ml/1 tbsp baking powder
115g/4oz/½ cup caster sugar
1 egg
250ml/8fl oz/1 cup buttermilk
60ml/4 tbsp sunflower oil
150g/5oz raspberries

1 Preheat the oven to 200°C/400°F/ Gas 6. Arrange 12 paper cake cases in a deep muffin tin. Sift the flour and baking powder into a mixing bowl, stir in the sugar, then make a well in the centre.

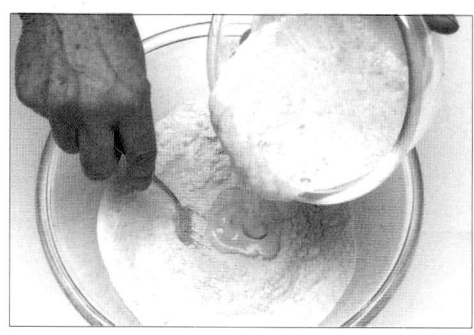

2 Mix the egg, buttermilk and sunflower oil together in a bowl, pour into the flour mixture and mix quickly.

3 Add the raspberries and lightly fold in with a metal spoon. Spoon the mixture into the paper cases.

4 Bake the muffins for 20–25 minutes until golden brown and firm in the middle. Transfer to a wire rack and serve warm or cold.

Spiced Banana Muffins

These light and nutritious muffins include banana for added fibre, and make a tasty tea-time treat. If liked, slice off the tops and fill with jam.

INGREDIENTS

Makes 12
75g/3oz/²⁄₃ cup plain wholemeal flour
50g/2oz/¹⁄₂ cup plain white flour
10ml/2 tsp baking powder
pinch of salt
5ml/1 tsp mixed spice
40g/1¹⁄₂oz/¹⁄₄ cup soft light brown sugar
50g/2oz/¹⁄₄ cup polyunsaturated
  margarine
1 egg, beaten
150ml/¹⁄₄ pint/²⁄₃ cup semi-skimmed
  milk
grated rind of 1 orange
1 ripe banana
20g/³⁄₄oz/¹⁄₄ cup porridge oats
20g/³⁄₄oz/scant ¹⁄₄ cup chopped
  hazelnuts

1 Preheat the oven to 200°C/400°F/ Gas 6. Line a muffin tin with 12 large paper cake cases. Sift together both flours, the baking powder, salt and mixed spice into a bowl, then tip the bran remaining in the sieve into the bowl. Stir in the sugar.

2 Melt the margarine and pour it into a mixing bowl. Cool slightly, then beat in the egg, milk and grated orange rind.

3 Gently fold in the dry ingredients. Mash the banana with a fork, then stir it gently into the mixture, being careful not to overmix.

4 Spoon the mixture into the paper cases. Combine the oats and hazelnuts and sprinkle a little of the mixture over each muffin.

5 Bake for 20 minutes until the muffins are well risen and golden, and a skewer inserted in the centre comes out clean. Transfer to a wire rack and serve warm or cold.

NUTRITION NOTES

Per muffin:	
Energy	110Kcals/465kJ
Fat	5g
Saturated Fat	1g
Cholesterol	17.5mg

BANANA AND APRICOT CHELSEA BUNS

These buns are old favourites given a low fat twist with a delectable fruit filling.

INGREDIENTS

Serves 9
90ml/6 tbsp warm skimmed milk
5ml/1 tsp dried yeast
pinch of sugar
225g/8oz/2 cups strong plain flour
10ml/2 tsp mixed spice
2.5ml/½ tsp salt
50g/2oz/¼ cup caster sugar
25g/1oz/2 tbsp soft margarine
1 egg

For the filling
1 large ripe banana
175g/6oz/1 cup ready-to-eat dried apricots
30ml/2 tbsp light muscovado sugar

For the glaze
30ml/2 tbsp caster sugar
30ml/2 tbsp water

COOK'S TIP
Do not leave the buns in the tins for too long, or the glaze will stick to the sides, making them very difficult to remove.

NUTRITION NOTES

Per bun:
Energy	214Kcals/901kJ
Fat	3.18g
Saturated Fat	0.63g
Cholesterol	21.59mg
Fibre	2.18g

1 Lightly grease an 18cm/7in square tin. Put the warm milk in a jug and sprinkle the yeast on top. Add a pinch of sugar to help activate the yeast, mix well and leave for 30 minutes.

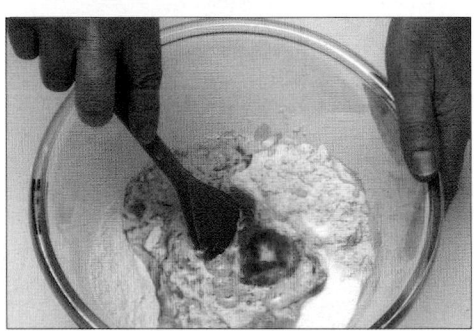

2 Sift the flour, spice and salt into a mixing bowl. Stir in the caster sugar, rub in the margarine, then stir in the yeast mixture and the egg. Gradually mix in the flour to make a soft dough, adding extra milk if needed.

3 Turn out the dough on to a floured surface and knead for 5 minutes until smooth and elastic. Return the dough to the clean bowl, cover with a damp dish towel and leave in a warm place for about 2 hours, until doubled in bulk.

4 To prepare the filling, mash the banana in a bowl. Using scissors, snip the apricots into pieces, then stir into the banana with the sugar.

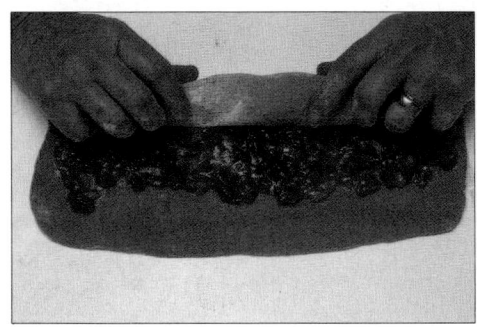

5 Knead the dough on a floured surface for 2 minutes, then roll out to a 30 x 23cm/12 x 9in rectangle. Spread the banana and apricot filling over the dough and roll up lengthways like a Swiss roll, with the join underneath.

6 Cut the roll into 9 buns. Place, cut side down, in the tin, cover and leave to rise for 30 minutes. Preheat the oven to 200°C/400°F/Gas 6 and bake for 20–25 minutes. Meanwhile, mix the caster sugar and water in a small saucepan. Heat, stirring, until dissolved, then boil for 2 minutes. Brush the glaze over the buns while still hot.

OATY CRISPS

These biscuits are very crisp and crunchy – ideal to serve with morning coffee.

INGREDIENTS

Makes 18
175g/6oz/1¾ cups rolled oats
75g/3oz/½ cup light muscovado
   sugar
1 egg
60ml/4 tbsp sunflower oil
30ml/2 tbsp malt extract

NUTRITION NOTES

Per portion:
Energy	86Kcals/360kJ
Fat	3.59g
Saturated Fat	0.57g
Cholesterol	10.7mg
Fibre	0.66g

1 Preheat the oven to 190°C/375°F/ Gas 5. Lightly grease two baking sheets. Mix the rolled oats and sugar in a bowl, breaking up any lumps in the sugar. Add the egg, sunflower oil and malt extract, mix well, then leave to soak for 15 minutes.

2 Using a teaspoon, place small heaps of the mixture well apart on the prepared baking sheets. Press the heaps into 7.5cm/3in rounds with the back of a dampened fork.

3 Bake the biscuits for 10–15 minutes until golden brown. Leave them to cool for 1 minute, then remove with a palette knife and cool on a wire rack.

COOK'S TIP
To give these biscuits a coarser texture, substitute jumbo oats for some or all of the rolled oats. Once cool, store the biscuits in an airtight container to keep them as crisp and fresh as possible.

OATCAKES

Try serving these oatcakes with reduced fat hard cheeses. They are delicious topped with thick honey for breakfast.

INGREDIENTS

Makes 8
175g/6oz/1 cup medium oatmeal, plus
   extra for sprinkling
2.5ml/½ tsp salt
pinch of bicarbonate of soda
15g/½oz/1 tbsp butter
75ml/5 tbsp water

1 Preheat the oven to 150°C/300°F/ Gas 2. Mix the oatmeal with the salt and bicarbonate of soda in a bowl.

2 Melt the butter with the water in a small saucepan. Bring to the boil, then add to the oatmeal mixture and mix to a moist dough.

> COOK'S TIP
> To achieve a neat round, place a 25cm/10in cake board or plate on top of the oatcake. Cut away any excess dough with a palette knife.

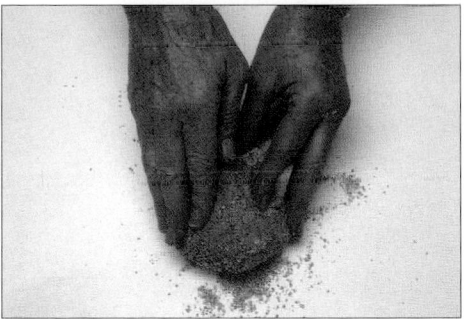

3 Turn the dough on to a surface sprinkled with oatmeal and knead to a smooth ball. Turn a large baking sheet upside-down, grease it, sprinkle it lightly with oatmeal and place the ball of dough on top. Sprinkle the dough with oatmeal, then roll out to a 25cm/10in round.

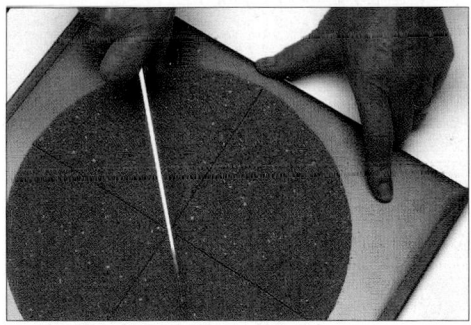

4 Cut the round into eight sections, ease them apart slightly and bake for about 50–60 minutes until crisp. Leave to cool on the baking sheet, then remove the oatcakes with a palette knife.

NUTRITION NOTES

Per portion:
Energy	102Kcals/427kJ
Fat	3.43g
Saturated Fat	0.66g
Cholesterol	0.13mg
Fibre	1.49g

BREADS AND TEABREADS

Breads and teabreads can be ideal low fat snacks at any time of day. Bread is the perfect accompaniment to many meals, and moist, flavourful teabread, served with a warm beverage, is a delightful treat. Among the appetizing selection of recipes presented here are Rosemary and Sea Salt Focaccia, Parma Ham and Parmesan Bread, Pear and Sultana Teabread and Banana and Cardamom Bread.

ROSEMARY AND SEA SALT FOCACCIA

Focaccia is an Italian flat bread made with olive oil. Here it is given added flavour with rosemary and coarse sea salt.

INGREDIENTS

Serves 8

350g/12oz/3 cups plain flour
2.5ml/1/2 tsp salt
10ml/2 tsp easy-blend dried yeast
about 250ml/8fl oz/1 cup
   lukewarm water
45ml/3 tbsp olive oil
1 small red onion
leaves from 1 large rosemary sprig
5ml/1 tsp coarse sea salt
oil, for greasing

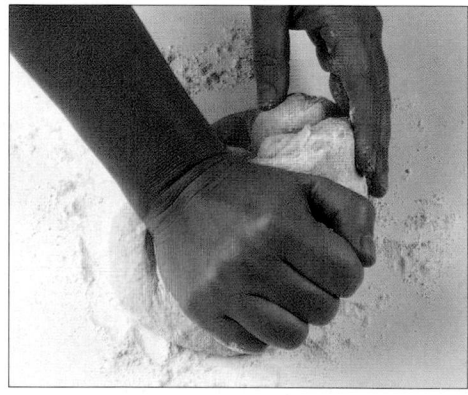

1 Sift the flour and salt into a large mixing bowl. Stir in the yeast, then make a well in the middle of the dry ingredients. Pour in the water and 30ml/2 tbsp of the oil. Mix well, adding a little more water if the mixture seems too dry.

COOK'S TIP
Use flavoured olive oil, such as chilli or herb oil, for extra flavour. Wholemeal flour or a mixture of wholemeal and white flour works well with this recipe.

2 Turn the dough on to a lightly floured surface and knead for about 10 minutes until smooth and elastic.

3 Place the dough in a greased bowl, cover and leave in a warm place for about 1 hour until doubled in size. Knock back and knead the dough for 2–3 minutes.

4 Meanwhile, preheat the oven to 220°C/425°F/Gas 7. Roll out the dough to a large circle about 1cm/1/2in thick, and transfer to a greased baking sheet. Brush with the remaining oil.

5 Halve the onion and slice it into thin wedges. Sprinkle over the dough, with the rosemary and sea salt, pressing lightly.

6 Using a finger, make deep indentations in the dough. Cover the surface with greased clear film, then leave to rise in a warm place for 30 minutes. Remove the clear film and bake for 25–30 minutes until golden.

NUTRITION NOTES	
Per portion:	
Energy	191Kcals/807kJ
Fat	4.72g
Saturated Fat	0.68g
Cholesterol	0
Fibre	1.46g

OLIVE AND OREGANO BREAD

This is an excellent accompaniment to all salads and is particularly good served warm.

INGREDIENTS

Serves 8–10
300ml/10fl oz/1¼ cups warm water
5ml/1 tsp dried yeast
pinch of sugar
15ml/1 tbsp olive oil
1 onion, chopped
450g/1lb/4 cups strong white flour
5ml/1 tsp salt
1.5ml/¼ tsp black pepper
50g/2oz/⅓ cup stoned black olives, roughly chopped
15ml/1 tbsp black olive paste
15ml/1 tbsp chopped fresh oregano
15ml/1 tbsp chopped fresh parsley

NUTRITION NOTES

Per portion:	
Energy	202Kcals/847kJ
Fat	3.28g
Saturated Fat	0.46g
Cholesterol	0
Fibre	22.13g

1 Put half the warm water in a jug. Sprinkle the yeast on top. Add the sugar, mix well and leave to stand for 10 minutes.

2 Heat the olive oil in a small frying pan and fry the onion gently until golden brown.

3 Sift the flour into a mixing bowl with the salt and pepper. Make a well in the centre. Add the yeast mixture, the fried onion (with the oil), the olives, olive paste, herbs and remaining water. Gradually incorporate the flour and mix to a soft dough, adding a little extra water if necessary.

4 Turn the dough on to a floured surface and knead for 5 minutes until smooth and elastic. Place in a mixing bowl, cover with a damp dish towel and leave in a warm place to rise for about 2 hours until the dough has doubled in bulk. Lightly grease a baking sheet.

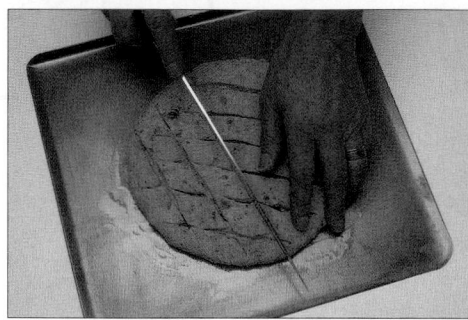

5 Turn the dough on to a floured surface and knead again for a few minutes. Shape into a 20cm/8in round and place on the prepared baking sheet. Using a large sharp knife, make crisscross cuts over the top. Cover and leave in a warm place for 30 minutes until well risen. Preheat the oven to 220°C/425°F/Gas 7.

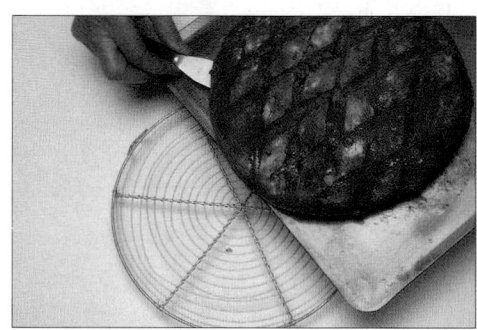

6 Dust the loaf with a little flour. Bake for 10 minutes, then lower the oven temperature to 200°C/400°F/Gas 6. Bake for 20 minutes more, or until the loaf sounds hollow when tapped underneath. Transfer to a wire rack and allow to cool slightly before serving.

COOK'S TIP
If fresh herbs are not available, use 5–10 ml/1–2 tsp dried herbs instead. Omit the olives and olive paste and use chopped sun-dried tomatoes and sun-dried tomato paste, for a tasty change.

Rye Bread

Rye bread is popular in northern Europe and makes an excellent base for open sandwiches – add a low fat topping of your choice.

INGREDIENTS

Serves 16
350g/12oz/3 cups wholemeal flour
225g/8oz/2 cups rye flour
115g/4oz/1 cup strong white flour
7.5ml/1½ tsp salt
30ml/2 tbsp caraway seeds
475ml/16fl oz/2 cups warm water
10ml/2 tsp dried yeast
pinch of sugar
30ml/2 tbsp molasses

1 Put the flours and salt in a bowl. Set aside 5ml/1 tsp of the caraway seeds and add the rest to the bowl.

2 Put half the water in a jug. Sprinkle the yeast on top. Add the sugar, mix well and leave for 10 minutes.

3 Make a well in the flour mixture, then add the yeast mixture with the molasses and the remaining water. Gradually incorporate the flour and mix to a soft dough, adding a little water if necessary.

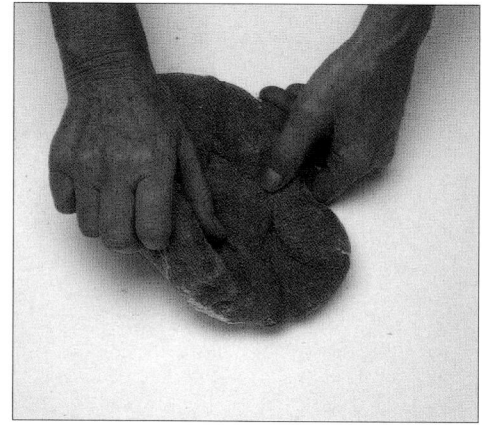

4 Turn the dough on to a floured surface and knead for 5 minutes until smooth and elastic. Return to the clean bowl, cover with a damp dish towel and leave in a warm place for about 2 hours until doubled in bulk. Grease a baking sheet.

NUTRITION NOTES

Per portion:	
Energy	156Kcals/655kJ
Fat	1.2g
Saturated Fat	0.05g
Cholesterol	0
Fibre	4.53g

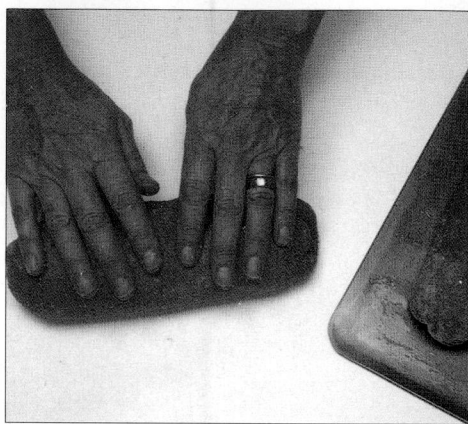

5 Turn the dough on to a floured surface and knead for 2 minutes. Divide the dough in half, then shape into two 23cm/9in long oval loaves. Flatten the loaves slightly and place them on a baking sheet.

6 Brush the loaves with water and sprinkle with the remaining caraway seeds. Cover and leave in a warm place for about 40 minutes until well risen. Preheat the oven to 200°C/400°F/Gas 6. Bake the loaves for 30 minutes or until they sound hollow when tapped underneath. Cool on a wire rack. Serve the bread plain, or slice and add a low fat topping.

SODA BREAD

Finding the bread bin empty need never be a problem again when your repertoire includes a recipe for soda bread. It takes only a few minutes to make and needs no rising or proving. If possible, eat soda bread while still warm from the oven as it does not keep well.

INGREDIENTS

Serves 8
450g/1lb/4 cups plain flour
5ml/1 tsp salt
5ml/1 tsp bicarbonate of soda
5ml/1 tsp cream of tartar
350ml/12fl oz/1½ cups buttermilk

1 Preheat the oven to 220°C/425°F/ Gas 7. Flour a baking sheet. Sift all the dry ingredients into a mixing bowl and make a small well in the centre.

2 Add the buttermilk and mix quickly to a soft dough. Turn on to a floured surface and knead lightly. Shape into a round about 18cm/7in across and put on the baking sheet.

3 Cut a deep cross on top of the loaf and sprinkle with a little flour. Bake for 25–30 minutes, then transfer the soda bread to a wire rack to cool.

COOK'S TIP
Soda bread needs a light hand. The ingredients should be bound together quickly in the bowl and kneaded very briefly. The aim is to get rid of the largest cracks, as the dough will become tough if it is handled for too long.

NUTRITION NOTES
Per portion:

Energy	230Kcals/967kJ
Fat	1.03g
Saturated Fat	0.24g
Cholesterol	0.88mg
Fibre	1.94g

PEAR AND SULTANA TEABREAD

This is an ideal teabread to make when pears are plentiful – an excellent use for windfalls.

Serves 6–8
25g/1oz/¼ cup rolled oats
50g/2oz/¼ cup light muscovado sugar
30ml/2 tbsp pear or apple juice
30ml/2 tbsp sunflower oil
1 large or 2 small pears
115g/4oz/1 cup self-raising flour
115g/4oz/¾ cup sultanas
2.5ml/½ tsp baking powder
10ml/2 tsp mixed spice
1 egg

1 Preheat the oven to 180°C/350°F/ Gas 4. Grease and line a 450g/1lb loaf tin with non-stick baking paper. Put the oats in a bowl with the sugar, pour over the pear or apple juice and oil, mix well and leave to stand for 15 minutes.

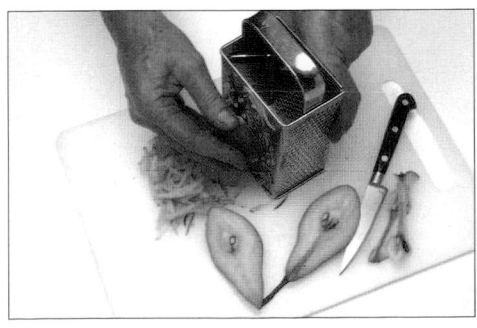

2 Quarter, core and coarsely grate the pear(s). Add to the oat mixture with the flour, sultanas, baking powder, mixed spice and egg, then mix together thoroughly.

3 Spoon the mixture into the prepared loaf tin and level the top. Bake for 50–60 minutes or until a skewer inserted into the centre comes out clean.

COOK'S TIP
Health food shops sell concentrated pear and apple juice, ready for diluting as required.

4 Transfer the teabread on to a wire rack and peel off the lining paper. Leave to cool completely.

NUTRITION NOTES

Per portion:	
Energy	200Kcals/814kJ
Fat	4.61g
Saturated Fat	0.79g
Cholesterol	27.50mg
Fibre	1.39g

PARMA HAM AND PARMESAN BREAD

This nourishing bread is almost a meal in itself.

INGREDIENTS

Serves 8

225g/8oz/2 cups self-raising wholemeal
   flour
225g/8oz/2 cups self-raising white flour
5ml/1 tsp baking powder
5ml/1 tsp salt
5ml/1 tsp black pepper
75g/3oz Parma ham
25g/1oz/2 tbsp freshly grated Parmesan
   cheese
30ml/2 tbsp chopped fresh parsley
45ml/3 tbsp Meaux mustard
350ml/12fl oz/1½ cups buttermilk
skimmed milk, to glaze

NUTRITION NOTES

Per portion:
Energy	250Kcals/1053kJ
Fat	3.65g
Saturated Fat	1.30g
Cholesterol	7.09mg
Fibre	3.81g

1 Preheat the oven to 200°C/400°F/ Gas 6. Flour a baking sheet. Place the wholemeal flour in a bowl and sift in the white flour, baking powder and salt. Add the pepper and the ham. Set aside about 15ml/1 tbsp of the grated Parmesan and stir the rest into the flour mixture with the parsley. Make a well in the centre.

2 Mix the mustard and buttermilk, pour into the flour and quickly mix to a soft dough.

3 Turn the dough on to a floured surface and knead briefly. Shape into an oval loaf, brush with milk and sprinkle with the Parmesan cheese. Put the loaf on the prepared baking sheet.

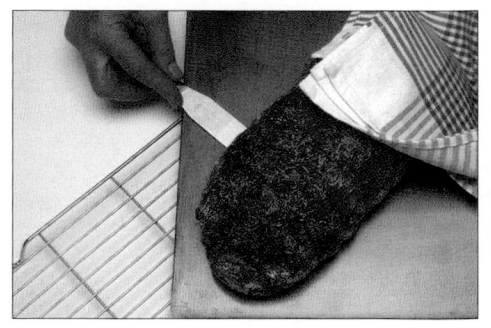

4 Bake the loaf for 25–30 minutes. Allow to cool before serving.

CARAWAY BREAD STICKS

Ideal to nibble with drinks, these can be made with all sorts of other seeds – try cumin seeds, poppy seeds or celery seeds.

INGREDIENTS

Makes about 20
150ml/¼ pint/⅔ cup warm water
2.5ml/½ tsp dried yeast
pinch of sugar
225g/8oz/2 cups plain flour
2.5ml/½ tsp salt
10ml/2 tsp caraway seeds

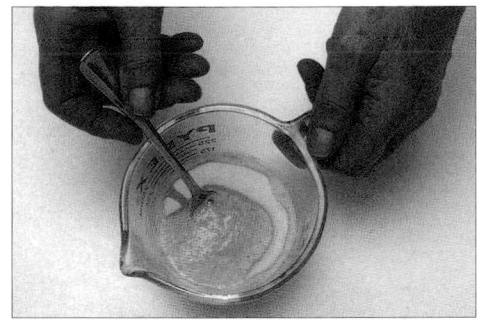

1 Grease two baking sheets. Put the warm water in a jug. Sprinkle the yeast on top. Add the sugar, mix well and leave for 10 minutes.

2 Sift the flour and salt into a mixing bowl, stir in the caraway seeds and make a well in the centre. Add the yeast mixture and gradually incorporate the flour to make a soft dough, adding a little water if necessary.

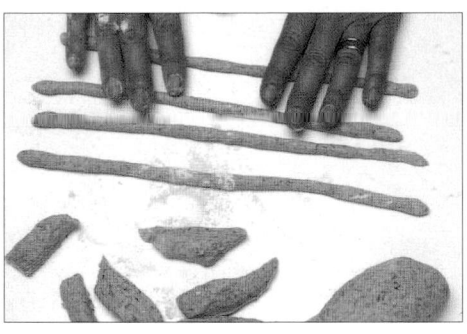

3 Preheat the oven to 200°C/425°F/ Gas 7. Turn the dough on to a lightly floured surface and knead for 5 minutes until smooth. Divide the mixture into 20 pieces and roll each into a 30cm/12in stick.

4 Arrange the sticks on the baking sheets, leaving room to allow for rising.

5 Bake the bread sticks for about 10–12 minutes until golden brown. Cool on the baking sheets.

NUTRITION NOTES	
Per portion:	
Energy	45Kcals/189kJ
Fat	0.24g
Saturated Fat	0.02g
Cholesterol	0
Fibre	0.3g

CHEESE AND ONION HERB STICKS

An extremely tasty bread which is very good with soups or salads. Use an extra-strong cheese to give plenty of flavour without piling on the fat.

INGREDIENTS

Makes 2 sticks, each serving 4–6
300ml/½ pint/1¼ cups warm water
5ml/1 tsp dried yeast
pinch of sugar
15ml/1 tbsp sunflower oil
1 red onion, finely chopped
450g/1lb/4 cups strong white flour
5ml/1 tsp salt
5ml/1 tsp dry mustard
45ml/3 tbsp chopped fresh herbs, such
   as thyme, parsley, marjoram or sage
75g/3oz/¾ cup grated reduced fat
   Cheddar cheese

NUTRITION NOTES

Per portion:	
Energy	210Kcals/882kJ
Fat	3.16g
Saturated Fat	0.25g
Cholesterol	3.22mg
Fibre	1.79g

COOK'S TIP
To make Onion and Coriander Sticks, omit the cheese, herbs and mustard. Add 15ml/1 tbsp ground coriander and 45ml/3 tbsp chopped fresh coriander instead.

1 Put the water in a jug. Sprinkle the yeast on top. Add the sugar, mix well and leave for 10 minutes.

2 Heat the oil in a small frying pan and fry the onion until it is well coloured.

3 Stir the flour, salt and mustard into a mixing bowl, then add the herbs. Set aside 30ml/2 tbsp of the cheese. Stir the rest into the flour mixture and make a well in the centre. Add the yeast mixture with the fried onions and oil, then gradually incorporate the flour and mix to a soft dough, adding extra water if necessary.

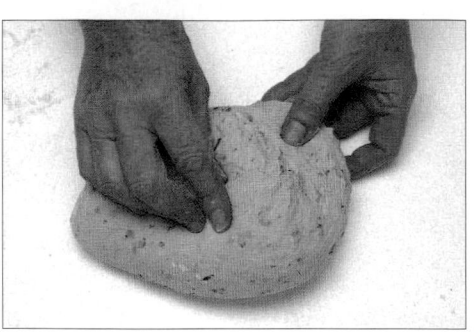

4 Turn the dough on to a floured surface and knead for 5 minutes until smooth and elastic. Return to the clean bowl, cover with a damp dish towel and leave in a warm place to rise for about 2 hours until doubled in bulk. Lightly grease two baking sheets.

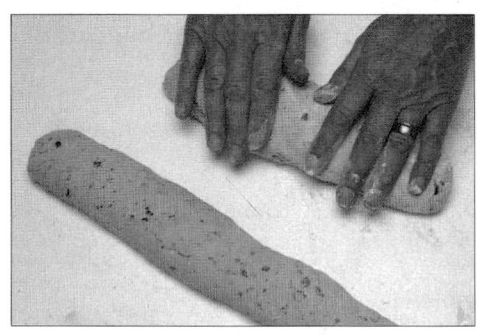

5 Turn the dough on to a floured surface, knead briefly, then divide the mixture in half and roll each piece into a 30cm/12in long stick. Place each stick on a baking sheet and make diagonal cuts along the top.

6 Sprinkle the sticks with the reserved cheese. Cover and leave for 30 minutes until well risen. Preheat the oven to 220°C/425°F/Gas 7. Bake the sticks for 25 minutes or until they sound hollow when tapped underneath.

GRANARY BAPS

These make excellent picnic fare, filled with cottage cheese, tuna, salad and low fat mayonnaise. They are also very good served warm with soup.

INGREDIENTS

Makes 8
300ml/¹/₂ pint/1¹/₄ cups warm water
5ml/1 tsp dried yeast
pinch of sugar
450g/1lb/4 cups malted brown flour
5ml/1 tsp salt
15ml/1 tbsp malt extract
15ml/1 tbsp rolled oats

NUTRITION NOTES

Per portion:
Energy	223Kcals/939kJ
Fat	1.14g
Saturated Fat	0.16g
Cholesterol	0
Fibre	3.10g

COOK'S TIP
To make a large loaf, shape the dough into a round, flatten it slightly and bake for 30–40 minutes. Test by tapping the base of the loaf – if it sounds hollow, it is cooked.

1 Put half the warm water in a jug. Sprinkle in the yeast. Add the sugar, mix well and leave for 10 minutes.

2 Put the malted brown flour and salt in a mixing bowl and make a well in the centre. Add the yeast mixture with the malt extract and the remaining water. Gradually incorporate the flour and mix to a soft dough.

3 Turn the dough on to a floured surface and knead for 5 minutes until smooth and elastic. Return to the clean bowl, cover with a damp dish towel and leave in a warm place to rise for about 2 hours until doubled in bulk.

4 Lightly grease a large baking sheet. Turn the dough on to a floured surface, knead for 2 minutes, then divide into eight pieces. Shape the pieces into balls and flatten them with the palm of your hand to make neat 10cm/4in rounds.

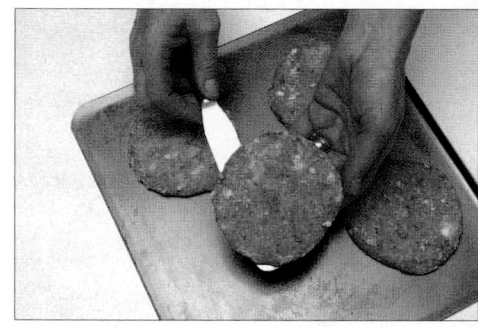

5 Place the rounds on the prepared baking sheet, cover loosely with a large plastic bag (ballooning it to trap the air inside), and leave to stand in a warm place until the baps are well risen. Preheat the oven to 220°C/425°F/Gas 7.

6 Brush the baps with water, sprinkle with the oats and bake for about 20–25 minutes or until they sound hollow when tapped underneath. Cool on a wire rack, then serve with the low fat filling of your choice.

POPPY SEED ROLLS

Pile these soft rolls in a basket and serve them for breakfast or with dinner.

INGREDIENTS

Makes 12
*300ml/¹/₂ pint/1¹/₄ cups warm
  skimmed milk*
5ml/1 tsp dried yeast
pinch of sugar
450g/1lb/4 cups strong white flour
5ml/1 tsp salt
1 egg, lightly beaten

For the topping
1 egg, beaten
poppy seeds

NUTRITION NOTES

Per portion:

Energy	160Kcals/674kJ
Fat	2.42g
Saturated Fat	0.46g
Cholesterol	32.58mg
Fibre	1.16g

1 Put half the warm milk in a small bowl. Sprinkle the yeast on top. Add the sugar, mix well and leave for 30 minutes.

2 Sift the flour and salt into a mixing bowl. Make a well in the centre and pour in the yeast mixture and the egg. Gradually incorporate the flour, adding enough of the remaining milk to mix to a soft dough.

3 Turn the dough on to a floured surface and knead for 5 minutes until smooth and elastic. Return to the clean bowl, cover with a damp dish towel and leave in a warm place to rise for about 1 hour until doubled in bulk.

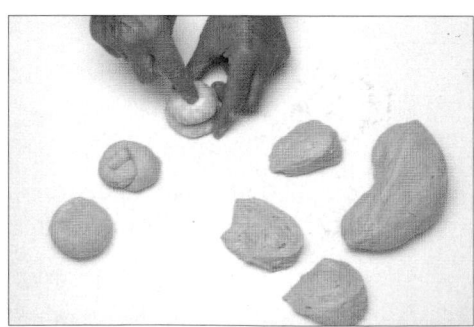

4 Lightly grease two baking sheets. Turn the dough on to a floured surface. Knead for 2 minutes, then cut into 12 pieces and shape into rolls.

5 Place the rolls on the prepared baking sheets, cover loosely with a large plastic bag (ballooning it to trap the air inside) and leave to stand in a warm place until the rolls have risen well. Preheat the oven to 220°C/425°F/Gas 7.

6 Glaze the rolls with beaten egg, sprinkle with poppy seeds and bake for 12–15 minutes until golden brown. Transfer to a wire rack to cool.

COOK'S TIP

Use easy-blend dried yeast if you prefer. Add it directly to the dry ingredients and mix with hand-hot milk. The rolls will only require one rising (see package instructions). Vary the toppings. Linseed, sesame seeds and caraway seeds are all good; try adding caraway seeds to the dough, too, for extra flavour.

BANANA AND CARDAMOM BREAD

The combination of banana and cardamom is delicious in this soft-textured moist loaf. It is perfect for tea time, served with low fat spread and jam. No fat is used or needed to make this delicious loaf, creating a healthy low fat bread for all to enjoy.

INGREDIENTS

Serves 6

150ml/¼ pint/⅔ cup warm water
5ml/1 tsp dried yeast
pinch of sugar
10 cardamom pods
400g/14oz/3½ cups strong white flour
5ml/1 tsp salt
30ml/2 tbsp malt extract
2 ripe bananas, mashed
5ml/1 tsp sesame seeds

1 Put the warm water in a small bowl. Sprinkle the yeast on top. Add the sugar, mix well and leave for 10 minutes.

2 Split the cardamom pods. Remove the seeds and chop them finely.

3 Sift the flour and salt into a mixing bowl and make a well in the centre. Add the yeast mixture with the malt extract, chopped cardamom seeds and bananas.

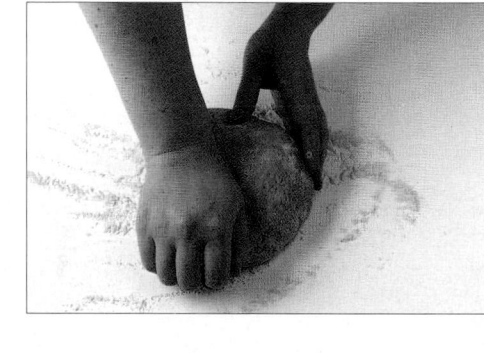

4 Gradually incorporate the flour and mix to a soft dough, adding a little extra water if necessary. Turn the dough on to a floured surface and knead for about 5 minutes until smooth and elastic. Return to the clean bowl, cover with a damp dish towel and leave to rise for about 2 hours until doubled in bulk.

NUTRITION NOTES

Per portion:

Energy	299Kcals/1254kJ
Fat	1.55g
Saturated Fat	0.23g
Cholesterol	0
Fibre	2.65g

5 Grease a baking sheet. Turn the dough on to a floured surface, knead briefly, then divide into three and shape into a plait. Place the plait on the baking sheet and cover loosely with a plastic bag (ballooning it to trap the air). Leave until well risen. Preheat the oven to 220°C/425°F/Gas 7.

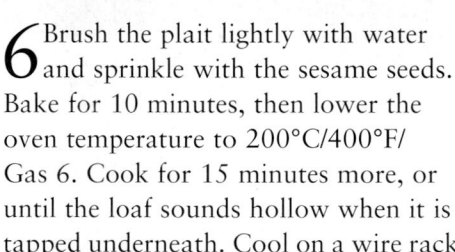

6 Brush the plait lightly with water and sprinkle with the sesame seeds. Bake for 10 minutes, then lower the oven temperature to 200°C/400°F/Gas 6. Cook for 15 minutes more, or until the loaf sounds hollow when it is tapped underneath. Cool on a wire rack.

COOK'S TIP
Make sure the bananas are really ripe, so that they impart maximum flavour to the bread. If you prefer, place the dough in one piece in a 450g/1lb loaf tin and bake for an extra 5 minutes. As well as being low in fat, bananas are a good source of potassium, therefore making an ideal nutritious, low fat snack.

SWEDISH SULTANA BREAD

A lightly sweetened fruit bread that is delicious served warm. It is also excellent toasted and topped with low fat spread.

INGREDIENTS

Serves 8–10
150ml/¼ pint/⅔ cup warm water
5ml/1 tsp dried yeast
15ml/1 tbsp clear honey
225g/8oz/2 cups wholemeal flour
225g/8oz/2 cups strong white flour
5ml/1 tsp salt
115g/4oz/⅔ cup sultanas
50g/2oz/½ cup walnuts, finely chopped
175ml/6fl oz/¾ cup warm skimmed milk, plus extra for glazing

NUTRITION NOTES

Per portion:	
Energy	273Kcals/1145kJ
Fat	4.86g
Saturated Fat	0.57g
Cholesterol	0.39mg
Fibre	3.83g

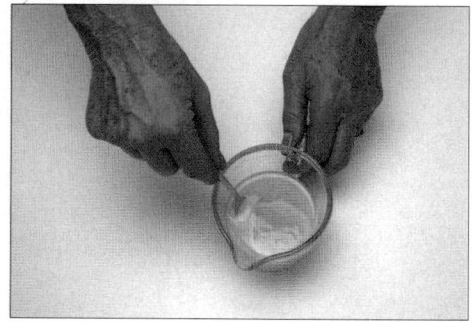

1 Put the water in a small jug. Sprinkle the yeast on top. Add a few drops of the honey to help activate the yeast, mix well and leave to stand for 10 minutes.

2 Put the flours in a mixing bowl with the salt and sultanas. Set aside 15ml/1 tbsp of the walnuts and add the rest to the bowl. Mix together lightly and make a well in the centre.

3 Add the yeast mixture to the flour mixture with the milk and remaining honey. Gradually incorporate the flour, mixing to a soft dough; add a little extra water if you need to.

4 Turn the dough on to a floured surface and knead for 5 minutes until smooth and elastic. Return to the clean bowl, cover with a damp dish towel and leave in a warm place to rise for about 2 hours until doubled in bulk. Grease a baking sheet.

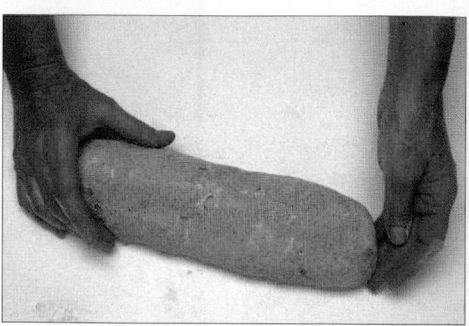

5 Turn the dough on to a floured surface and form into a 28cm/11in long sausage shape. Place on the baking sheet. Make some diagonal cuts down the whole length of the loaf.

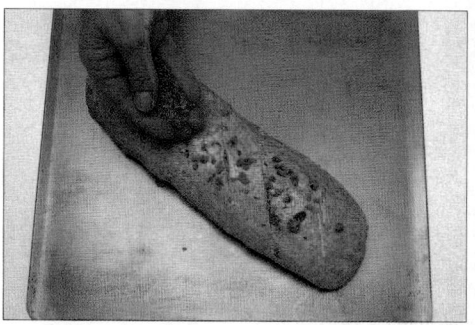

6 Brush the loaf with milk to glaze, sprinkle with the reserved walnuts and leave to rise for about 40 minutes. Preheat the oven to 220°C/425°F/ Gas 7. Bake the loaf for 10 minutes. Lower the oven temperature to 200°C/400°F/Gas 6 and bake for about 20 minutes more, or until the loaf sounds hollow when tapped underneath.

COOK'S TIP
To make Apple and Hazelnut Bread, replace the sultanas with two chopped eating apples and use chopped toasted hazelnuts instead of the walnuts. Add 5ml/1 tsp ground cinnamon with the flour.

Index

angel cake, 197
  chocolate and orange, 200
apple juice:
  sultana and couscous
    pudding, 153
apples:
  apple and blackberry terrine, 174
  apple and blackcurrant
    pancakes, 157
  apple and hazelnut bread, 250
  baked apples in honey and
    lemon, 156
  chunky apple bake, 154
  cinnamon apple gâteau, 202
  cool green fruit salad, 186
  date and apple muffins, 223
  fresh fig, apple and date
    salad, 46
  strawberry and apple
    crumble, 152
apricots:
  apricot delice, 166
  apricot glaze, 202
  apricot sponge bars, 207
  banana and apricot Chelsea
    buns, 226
  cinnamon and apricot
    soufflés, 158
  quick apricot whip, 176
asparagus:
  courgette and asparagus
    parcels, 121
  pasta primavera, 59
aubergines:
  aubergine salad, 140
  ratatouille pancakes, 126
  ratatouille penne bake, 65
  roasted Mediterranean
    vegetables, 125
autumn glory, 122

bamboo shoot salad, 141
banana leaves, baked fish in, 107
bananas:
  banana and apricot Chelsea
    buns, 226
  banana and cardamom
    bread, 248
  banana and gingerbread
    slices, 214
  chocolate and banana
    brownies, 209
  spiced banana muffins, 225

baps, granary, 244
barbecued chicken, 86
bass:
  steamed fish with chilli
    sauce, 104
bean curd (tofu):
  mango and ginger clouds, 169
  ratatouille penne bake, 65
  spinach and bean curd
    soup, 24
  tofu and green bean curry, 131
beans:
  bean purée with grilled
    chicory, 74
  cauliflower and bean soup, 31
  chilli bean bake, 72
  fruit and fibre salad, 138
  spaghetti with chilli bean
    sauce, 62
  spicy bean hot pot, 73
  vegetarian cassoulet, 132
beef:
  spaghetti Bolognese, 64
  Thai beef salad, 82
beetroot:
  beetroot soup with ravioli, 20
  red onion and beetroot
    soup, 30
biryani, vegetable, 76
biscuits:
  oatcakes, 229
  oaty crisps, 228
blackberries:
  apple and blackberry terrine, 174
blackcurrants:
  apple and blackcurrant
    pancakes, 157
blueberry and orange crêpe
  baskets, 160
blushing pears, 162
bread, recipes using:
  cheese and chutney toasties, 48
  chunky apple bake, 154
  devilled onions en croûte, 118
  fruity ham and French bread
    pizza, 70
  Parma ham and pepper
    pizzas, 49
breads, 231–46
  caraway bread sticks, 241
  cheese and onion herb sticks, 242
  granary baps, 244
  olive and oregano bread, 234
  onion and coriander sticks, 242
  Parma ham and Parmesan
    bread, 240
  poppy seed rolls, 246
  rosemary and sea salt
    focaccia, 232
  rye bread, 236
  soda bread, 238
brown rice salad with fruit, 143
brownies, chocolate and
  banana, 209
bulgur wheat salad with
  oranges, 142
  see also cracked wheat

buns, banana and apricot Chelsea,
  226
buttermilk:
  raspberry muffins, 224

cabbage:
  fruit and fibre salad, 138
cachumbar, 149
Cajun-style cod, 98
cakes, 165-214
  angel cake, 197
  banana and gingerbread
    slices, 214
  chocolate and banana
    brownies, 209
  chocolate and orange angel
    cake, 200
  cinnamon apple gâteau, 202
  Irish whiskey cake, 196
  lemon chiffon cake, 212
  peach Swiss roll, 210
  Tia Maria gâteau, 198
campanelle, hot spicy prawns
  with, 56
Campari:
  grapefruit salad with orange, 37
cannellini beans:
  bean purée with grilled
    chicory, 74
  spaghetti with chilli bean
    sauce, 62
  spicy bean hot pot, 73
caraway bread sticks, 241
cardamom:
  banana and cardamom
    bread, 248
carrots:
  carrot and coriander soup, 27
  chicken, carrot and leek
    parcels, 88
  fruit and fibre salad, 138
  pasta primavera, 59
  vegetable biryani, 76

cassoulet, vegetarian, 132
cauliflower:
  cauliflower and bean soup, 31
  vegetable biryani, 76
  vegetables à la Grecque, 124
cellophane noodles:
  prawn noodle salad, 148
cheese:
  cheese and chive scones, 221

cheese and chutney toasties, 48
cheese and onion herb sticks, 242
fruity ham and French bread
  pizza, 70
Parma ham and Parmesan bread,
  240
Parma ham and pepper
  pizzas, 49
potato gratin, 115
turkey and macaroni cheese, 52
cheese, soft:
  chunky apple bake, 154
  coffee sponge drops, 208
  fusilli with smoked trout, 55
  gooseberry cheese cooler, 170
  pasta primavera, 59
  raspberry vacherin, 184
  spaghetti alla carbonara, 69
  strawberry rose-petal
    pashka, 192
  Tia Maria gâteau, 198

Chelsea buns, banana and
  apricot, 226
cherries, dried:
  duck breast salad, 90
chick-peas:
  pasta with chick-pea sauce, 67
  spaghetti with chilli bean
    sauce, 62
chicken:
  barbecued chicken, 86
  chicken and coconut
    soup, 28
  chicken and pasta soup, 19
  chicken, carrot and leek
    parcels, 88
  fragrant chicken curry, 92
  stock, 24
  tandoori chicken kebabs, 87
  Thai chicken and vegetable
    stir-fry, 89
  Thai-style chicken salad, 146
chicory, bean purée with
  grilled, 74
chiffon cake, lemon, 212
chilled fresh tomato soup, 33
chillies, 131
  aubergine salad, 140
  baked fish in banana leaves, 107
  chicken and coconut
    soup, 28
  chilli bean bake, 72